Outsiders' Response
to European Integration

Outsiders' Response to European Integration

Edited by

Seev Hirsch & Tamar Almor

HANDELSHØJSKOLENS FORLAG
Distribution: Munksgaard International Publishers Ltd
Copenhagen

© by the authors and Handelshøjskolens Forlag 1996
Printed in Denmark 1996
Set in Plantin by ABK-Sats, Denmark
Printed by Reproset, Copenhagen
Cover designed by Kontrapunkt
Book designed by Jørn Ekstrøm

ISBN 87-16-13233-5

Series A
COPENHAGEN STUDIES IN ECONOMICS AND MANAGEMENT, NO. 7

Contents

Contributors
Their Affiliations
and Research Interest

Tamar Almor lecturers at The College of Management and at the Faculty of Management, The Leon Recanati Graduate School of Business Administration, Tel Aviv University, Israel (Ph.D., Tel Aviv University). Her research interests include strategic management and internationalization strategies of business firms.

Christian Bellak is a Lecturer in Economics at the University of Economics, Vienna, Austria. He was recently Visiting Research Fellow at the Helsinki School of Economics in Finland and at the University of Reading, UK. His main research interests: foreign direct investment, multinational enterprises and industrial policy *vis-à-vis* small countries.

Pontus Braunerhjelm is a Senior Research Fellow at The Institute for Economic and Social Research (IUI), Stockholm, and since 1993 also its vice president. He is associated with The Graduate Institute for international Studies, Geneva, at which he earned his Ph.D. At present, Pontus Braunerhjelm's research focuses on firm dynamics, in particular the implications of increased international footlooseness of firms on countries' production specialization, trade patterns and growth rates.

Robert Gärtner is a member of the research staff of the Department of Business Administration, Lund University. His research focuses on the implications of changes in the macroeconomic environment on corporate decision-making, and in particular on how the decision-making ultimately affects the value of the firm.

Philippe Gugler is currently at the Federal Office for Foreign Economic Affairs in Bern, Switzerland. In addition, he is also a Research Fellow and occasional lecturer at the Centre of Research in Spatial Economics of the University of Fribourg, Switzerland. He studied international production and transnational corporation strategies at the Graduate School of Management, Rutgers University, New Jersey, under the supervision of Professor John Dunning. His current research interests are in the areas of foreign direct investment, strategic alliances and competitiveness of small countries.

Seev Hirsch is Jaffee Professor of International Trade at the Leon Recanati Graduate School of Business Administration, Tel Aviv University, Israel. His research interests include internationalization strategies of business firms in small and open economies, international business theory and economic aspects of the Middle East peace process.

Lars Oxelheim is Professor International Business at Lund University. He is also a Senior Research Fellow at the Industrial Institute for Social and Economic Research in Stockholm. For the period 1988-1992, he was Professor of finance at the School of Economics and Commercial Law, Gothenburg University. His current research interest is in the area of corporate decision-making in an increasingly integrated world.

Introduction

This book is the outcome of a collaborative enterprise undertaken by members of a research network, established at the Danish Summer Research Institute. The Institute was directed by Professor Lauge Stetting, chairperson of the Institute of International Economics and Management of the Copenhagen Business School. Three two-week workshops were held by the Institute in Gilleleje, Denmark during the month of August in the years 1990, 1991 and 1992.

The purpose of the Institute was to bring together scholars from academic institutions around the world, to study and evaluate together different aspects of European integration. As might be expected, a major part of the discussions was devoted to Europe Ninety Two, the ambitious program outlined in the European Commission's White Paper of 1985, which set out to complete the European common market by the end of 1992.

One of the stated goals of the organizers was to encourage the formation of networks of scholars from different countries. It was expected that these networks would engage in research on the accelerating process of European economic integration and its implications for Union members and for outsiders.

This volume reports on the research performed by members of one of these networks, all of whom from countries that were not members of the Union on the first of January 1993. Four of the seven authors are from countries that, by the beginning of 1995, have joined the European Union: Christian Bellak (Austria); Pontus Braunerhjelm, Robert Gärtner and Lars Oxelheim (Sweden). The remaining three are from countries that remain outsiders: Philippe Gugler (Switzerland); Tamar Almor and Seev Hirsch (Israel).

The home countries of the authors share a number of additional characteristics: all are small in terms of their population, and all have intensive economic relations with the European Union (previously the European Community). Consequently, at the time of the formation of the network, all were concerned about the potentially negative effects that full economic integration within the European Union might have on the economies of outsiders. The title of this book reflects these common characteristics and concerns.

In the introductory chapter "Europe Ninety-Two: Effects on Outsiders", Tamar Almor and Seev Hirsch outline a model that analyzes the effects of Europe Nineteen Ninety-Two (EC92) on insiders and outsiders. The authors show that the competitive position of outsiders is expected to be adversely affected by EC92, even if the Union refrains from adopting the discriminatory measures commonly envisaged under the title of Fortress Europe. Reasoning that firms have the option of becoming insiders by establishing operating subsidiaries within the European Union, the authors develop a framework that predicts the effects of EC92 on the propensity of outsider firms to engage in direct investment in the European Union relative to other markets and relative to trade. The framework distinguishes between innovative, skill-intensive industries (Schumpeter industries) and mature, low-skill industries (Heckscher-Ohlin industries).

It is predicted that outsider firms will respond to EC92 by increasing foreign direct investment in the European Union relative to other markets, that foreign direct investment (FDI) in the European Union will grow in relation to exports and that the propensity of Schumpeter industries to invest in the European Union will be higher than that of Heckscher-Ohlin industries. These hypotheses are largely confirmed by an empirical analysis of Israel's international trade and foreign direct investment data.

The framework, which was first introduced by Tamar Almor and Seev Hirsch in the Institute's workshop of 1991, was employed by other members of the network, in analyzing the changes in international trade and investment flows that could be related to EC92.

In a short chapter entitled "Small Outsider Countries' Response to the EC 1992 Program; Some Stylized Facts" Lars Oxelheim and Robert Gärtner extend the empirical investigation to a number of other small outsider countries including Sweden, Norway, Finland and Austria. Their analysis shows that the last decade was characterized by a tremendous increase in the flows of foreign direct investment, both absolutely and in relation to exports. A large share of these flows was directed to the European Union in an apparent response to the challenges posed by EC92 and the possibility of Fortress Europe. The authors regard these flows as representing investment diversion which is analogous to the trade diverting effects of the formation of protectionist trading blocks. Fear of exclusion from lucrative European Union markets by public policies motivated by the spirit of Fortress Europe has caused firms to divert investments from home countries, even in those cases where they could be more efficiently employed in home markets.

The theme of Fortress Europe also crops up in Christian Bellak's chapter, "Foreign Direct Investment From Small States and Integration: Micro- and Macroeconomic Evidence from Austria". Examining the past experience of Austria *vis-à-vis* the European Union, Bellak assumes Fortress Europe as given, and examines the responses available to small outsiders. He distinguishes between macro- and microeconomic responses. At the macroeconomic level the options include lowering of trade barriers through arrangements of the kind that led to the European Economic Area Agreement. Another option that Austria (together with Sweden and Finland) eventually chose, was to join the European Union – thus nullifying the adverse effects of Fortress Europe by accepting all the rights and obligations of full membership.

Bellak's chapter deals extensively with microresponses, that is, the response of individual firms that can become insiders, regardless of the status of their home countries, by establishing operating subsidiaries within the European Union. Bellak argues that macro- and microresponses do not substitute each other. In fact, they complement each other in the sense that only by engaging in FDI in the major European Union markets can Austrian firms fully benefit from Austria's membership. Analyzing trends in incoming and outgoing FDI, the author shows that outgoing investments have far exceeded incoming ones since 1987. The timing of these flows, their magnitude and direction clearly indicate that they represent a response to EC92 and the associated threat of Fortress Europe.

The macro- and microeffects of EC92 on outsiders are further examined in the chapter "Structural Implications of the Investment Response by Swedish Multinational Firms to the EC92 Program" by Pontus Braunerhjelm and Lars Oxelheim. Using aggregate data on Swedish domestic and foreign investments during the period 1982 to 1992 the authors address a number of difficult questions: Is FDI a substitute for domestic investment? Does the EC92 divert investments from the home market to the European Union? Is there a systematic difference between the FDI behavior of the Heckscher-Ohlin and Schumpeter industries? Their answer to all three questions are positive: Foreign investments appear to substitute domestic investments; EC92 appears to have been responsible for shifting Swedish investments from the domestic market towards the European Union. This trend has been particularly strong in the Schumpeter industries.

In the following chapter "Home Country Effects From Outward FDI – A Regional Study of Changes in Production Patterns", Lars Oxelheim and Robert Gärtner ask similar questions. In this case, the geographic scope of the analysis is extended and covers Norway and Finland in addition to Sweden. Denmark, which unlike the other Scandinavian countries is a member of the European Union, is also included. The analysis turns from the macro to the micro level; it covers the production patterns of the ten largest industrial firms in the four countries. The patterns that emerge are mostly consistent with expectations based on the previous analyses. Growth in total value added and in total employment exceeded growth in domestic value added and employment in all four Nordic countries, during the 1982-1992 period. Patterns of change in the relative share of Heckscher-Ohlin and Schumpeter industries in value added was less uniform. The share of Schumpeter firms in domestic value added declined in Denmark and Sweden and increased in Finland and Norway. Their share in total value added increased in Denmark, while remaining unchanged in Finland and declining in both Sweden and Norway.

The contribution of Philippe Gugler, "European Integration and Uruguay Round Results on Trade in Services" provides a Swiss perspective of outsiders' response to European integration, emphasizing the important role of services. International transactions in most services had been severely restricted in the past, even between European Union members. EC92 called for far reaching intra-European Union liberalization measures in several services including financial services in which Switzerland has substantial interests. These measures, based largely on the principle of Mutual Recognition, enable firms from member countries to compete on equal terms with domestic firms, in all European Union markets.

Switzerland, which is known to have a highly efficient and internationally competitive service sector, is clearly concerned about the business-diverting effects of EC92. Unlike Austria, Finland and Sweden, Switzerland has opted to stay outside the European Union. Consequently, it seeks ways to minimize the prospect of Fortress Europe. To achieve this goal, Switzerland has been pursuing two parallel policies. Firstly, Switzerland has engaged in intensive bilateral negotiations with the European Union concerning conditions of access for its service firms. The second policy involves the strengthening of the General Agreement on Trade in Services (GATS). The GATS, which was recently established as part of the World Trade Organization, following the successful conclusion of the

Uruguay Round, is primarily concerned with liberalizing world trade in services.

Gugler's analysis leads him to conclude that the two options should be pursued simultaneously. Obligations assumed by the European Union under the rules of the GATS are unlikely to guarantee full National Treatment to Swiss firms. Bilateral negotiations, in which Switzerland has some powerful cards up its sleeves, can improve the terms on which Swiss service firms can compete in the European Union markets. Finally, the chapter stresses the FDI option open to individual firms. This option appears to be particularly important in the service sector which offers intangible products whose tradability depends on direct interaction between provider and user.

The chapters discussed thus far consider FDI as a typical response to EC92 by outsider firms seeking to cope with its challenges it poses in general and its adverse effects on market accessibility, in particular. In her paper, "Responding to Unification of the European Community: The Use of International Strategic Alliances by Outsiders" Tamar Almor examines another mode of response to EC92 by outsiders: joint ventures. To be sure, joint ventures, which form an important subgroup of strategic alliances, usually involve foreign direct investments. There are, however, other forms of international strategic alliances – for example, cooperation agreements and exchange of know-how, which do not necessarily require all parties to engage in FDI.

"International Strategic Alliances" notes Almor, "enable firms to establish a foothold in the European Union while exploiting the advantages of a partnership with an insider firm, thus becoming insiders". Almor's findings pertain to a fairly large sample of Israel-based international strategic alliances, all related to the European Union. Like the FDIs discussed in the previous chapters, the number of Israeli international strategic alliances was found to increase very substantially, following the announcement on EC92. Contrary to expectations Almor did not find that the proportion of Schumpeter firms engaged in the formation of international strategic alliances was higher than that of Heckscher-Ohlin firms. There was, however, an interesting difference in motivation. While Schumpeter firms regard the establishment of a strategic alliance with European Union firms as a mechanism for exploiting opportunities, Heckscher-Ohlin firms more often expect the alliance to be instrumental in countering the threats posed to outsiders by the completion of the Common Market.

Chapter 1:
Europe Ninety-Two:
Effects on Outsiders[1]

Seev Hirsch and Tamar Almor

Europe Ninety Two is the term used to describe the program that the European Union (formerly called the European Community) adopted so as to accelerate the completion of the Single European Market. The program, which was intended to reverse unfavorable trends in the Union's international competitive performance manifested by low rates of productivity growth and decline in world market shares of advanced products, consists of numerous measures intended to remove the impediments to complete economic integration. These include the abolition of border controls, amendment of technical regulations, opening of public procurement programs to all Union members, elimination of barriers to financial and business services, and numerous other steps to eliminate intra-Union barriers to the movement of goods, services, capital and people.

The Cecchini Report, and other studies conducted by or on behalf of the European Union, indicated that the steps taken to complete the European internal market would enhance the economic welfare of the Union's residents and would increase the growth rate of the EU's economies (Baldwin 1989; Cecchini, Catinat and Jacquemin 1988; Commission of the European Communities 1988). These studies enumerate the positive effects that the adoption of integrative measures is expected to have on the economies of the member countries. They distinguish between different types of gains: gains from removal of barriers affecting trade and overall production; gains from exploiting economies of scale; and gains from intensified competition – including the reduction of business inefficiencies and monopoly profits.

Clearly, not all economic actors stand to gain from the implementation of Europe Ninety Two (EC92). On the whole, European Union consumers will benefit from the intensified competition resulting from economic integration. European Union producers will also gain as a group,

---

[1] This chapter is based partly on Almor and Hirsch (1995).

although some will inevitably fare better than others. This chapter focuses on the effects of EC92 on a third group – the outsiders, or more specifically, producers located in countries not belonging to the European Union who seek to serve its markets.

The theoretical sections of this chapter examine two aspects of EC92: (1) the effect of EC92 on the relative competitive position of outsider firms, and (2) the response, by means of foreign direct investment (FDI) to EC92 by two groups of outsider firms: producers of mature products characterized by publicly available technologies, which we label Heckscher-Ohlin goods; and Schumpeter goods producers, that is, producers of technology-intensive products characterized by firm-specific, technical, marketing and managerial knowledge.

A number of empirically testable hypotheses regarding the FDI strategies of outsider firms are derived from the theoretical discussion. They concern geographic distribution, sectoral distribution, and changes over time in anticipation of EC92. These hypotheses are tested on data pertaining to Israeli firms during two time periods: 1984-1987 and 1988-1991.

I. Trade Creation, Trade Diversion and EC92

International trade theory teaches that economic integration in which some countries participate while others do not is not necessarily an unmitigated blessing to the world, or even to the parties forming the economic union, common market or free trade area (Viner 1947; Meade 1955). When the net benefits expected from partial economic integration are evaluated the gains from trade creation must be balanced against the losses from trade diversion. A cost benefit analysis of EC92 based on these concepts will show that even if the completion of the single market involves no new discriminatory moves against outsiders, it inevitably gives rise to both effects. Ceteris Paribus, the ratio of trade creation to trade diversion effects is likely to be higher in countries belonging to the integrating area than in countries remaining on the outside.

Trade creation takes place following the establishment of a free trade area (or higher forms of integration) when inefficient national firms of a member country are displaced by more efficient firms located in other countries belonging to the same free trade area. Despite the elimination of intra- European Union tariffs prior to EC92, numerous trade impediments remained, as the Cecchini Report so amply demonstrated. These provided protection to national firms, facing competition from foreign suppliers, even when the latter were based in countries belonging to the Union. One of the major goals of EC92 has been to achieve trade creation by removing the numerous non-tariff barriers facing insider firms.

Trade diversion takes place when relatively efficient outsider suppliers are displaced by less efficient insiders due to discriminatory measures imposed on the former. Textbook examples of trade diversion usually pertain to tariffs. Prior to the creation of the free trade area, tariff protection is too low to enable inefficient national producers to displace efficient outsiders. Creation of a free trade area eliminates tariffs between members, thus enabling the relatively efficient insider to displace the even more efficient outsider. EC92 can give rise to new trade diversion even if no new trade restrictions are imposed on outsiders.

International transactions are determined by relative rather then by absolute costs. Costs have numerous components that include the expenses of gaining market access. When the access costs of one supplier decrease in relation to the access costs of its competitor, the competitive position of the latter deteriorates. It is thus conceivable that changes in relative access costs generated by EC92 could prevent the export of goods to the European Union, even when the absolute costs of outside suppliers remain unchanged or decline. EC92 thus might give rise to trade diversion. This proposition is examined more formally below where the focus switches to the individual firm, the organism that transforms the abstract concept of comparative advantage, trade creation and trade diversion into actual flows of goods, services, capital and technology. Assuming that business firms are profit maximizers, we can construct models that are consistent with the concepts discussed above, and that predict the responses of insider and outsider firms to some of the provisions of EC92.

II. The Effects of EC92 on Outsider Firms: A Conceptual Framework

The EC92 process is ongoing. Many directives and other policy decisions pertaining to specific industries vary from case to case and, moreover, numerous directives have not yet been implemented or even approved. Consequently, it is difficult to speculate about the impact of EC92 on the competitive position of specific countries and industries. The following example illustrates, however, the effect on outsiders of a very important related policy – the elimination of border controls between members of the Union.

Border controls symbolize, perhaps more than other barriers, the changes brought about by the completion of the single European Market. The proliferation of border controls results in delays due to the time spent on filling in forms, on clearing customs and generally on the bureaucracy involved with complying with the rules and regulations governing the transfer of goods across national boundaries. Such activities add to the costs of doing business with foreign firms, thus protecting domestic firms against foreign competitors. This was amply demonstrated in the Cecchini Report, which estimated that the removal of internal border controls would increase the Union's Gross Domestic Product by as much as 0.4%, which amounts to about 8% of the total estimated gains expected from the completion of the single market. It is easy to demonstrate that this change would reduce the costs of outsiders but by a smaller margin than the costs of insiders, since the Union's external border controls would not be dismantled.

To illustrate this point, consider two plywood suppliers to a Frankfurt-based customer, one located in Israel and the other in Spain. The Israeli plywood would be shipped by sea from Haifa to Marseilles and transported over land to Frankfurt. With the elimination of border controls between France and Germany following EC92, the shipment from Israel would not delayed beyond Marseilles. The Israeli plywood exporter would therefore gain in absolute terms from the removal of border controls. However, the Spanish plywood exporter would benefit even more. Whereas before the implementation of EC92, his shipments to Germany would bear the cost of border crossings at the France-Spain and the France-Germany borders, after EC92, Spanish shipments to Germany would encounter no border controls at all. Consequently, in relative terms the Spanish exporter is better off in relation to the Israeli exporter. Worst off in our hypothetical example is the German domestic producer. Prior to EC92 it was protected against the Spanish and the Israeli suppliers by the existence of two border posts. After EC92 it would lose all border-related protection against the Spanish exporter, and its protection against the Israeli exporter would be diminished by the elimination of the France-Germany border posts. The German supplier would be, however, compensated in other European Union markets where it competes mainly against other domestic firms and where, following EC92, the latter lose the protection provided by border controls.

A superficial analysis of other policies associated with EC92 – for example, public procurement (Tovias 1990), technical regulation and trade in services (Hirsch 1990) – confirms the expectation that EC92 will benefit firms located inside the European Union more than firms located outside it. Since relative rather than absolute costs determine the competitive position of business firms, we must conclude that, ceteris paribus, the competitive position of outsiders is going to be adversely affected by EC92 – even if the Union rejects the principle of Fortress Europe .

The adverse effects of EC92 on outsiders will, as was noted above, vary by target market, by source country, by industry and even by firm. The relative intensity of these effects can nevertheless be generalized as shown in Figure 1. Consider four manufacturers located in four countries A, B and C (members of the European Union, that is, insiders) and R (a non-member or outsider). All firms are assumed to compete in each other's markets. EC92 affects access costs to the European Union markets by eliminating entry barriers faced by the A, B and C firms. The R firm, on the other hand, still encounters entry barriers, as it has to enter the European Union from the outside. Figure 1 illustrates the change in the competitive position of each of the four firms (henceforth labeled simply as A, B, C and R) in the three European Union markets following EC92.

The upper half of Figure 1 summarizes the changes in the competitive position of A in relation to B and C, the other insiders, and R – the outsider. The lower half shows the change in the competitive position of R in the three insiders' markets. A plus sign signifies an improvement, a minus sign – deterioration, a zero – no change, and brackets – a relatively small change in the competitive position of the firm.

Figure 1. Change in the relative competitive position of insiders and outsiders following the implementation of EC92.

		TARGET MARKET:		
		A	B	C
A'S POSITION RELATIVE TO:	B	-	+	0
	C	-	0	+
	R	(-)	+	+
R'S POSITION RELATIVE TO:	A	(+)	-	-
	B	-	(+)	-
	C	-	-	(+)

The first row illustrates the changes in A's competitive position *vis-à-vis* B's in A's, B's and C's domestic markets. The second and third rows illustrate the changes in the competitive position of A *vis-à-vis* C and R in A's, B's and C's domestic markets respectively. The following changes in the competitive position of the different firms are indicated: A's competitive position *vis-à-vis* B's, in A's home market deteriorates. As barriers to entry facing insiders in A's home market are eliminated, A's market is turned into a domestic market for B and C. While the competitive position in its home market deteriorates, A's competitive position *vis-à-vis* B and C in their respective home markets improves. A's competitive position *vis-à-vis* B's in C's domestic market and *vis-à-vis* C's in B's domestic market remains unchanged.

The effects of EC92 on the changes of the competitive position of B and C in their domestic and other European Union markets are symmetrical to those experienced by A, which are illustrated in the top part of Figure 1. We can generalize as follows: Insiders' competitive position in their home market *vis-à-vis* insiders from other European Union countries deteriorates. It also deteriorates *vis-à-vis* the outsiders, though by a smaller margin. Their competitive position in the home market of other insiders improves *vis-à-vis* domestic manufacturers and (though by a smaller margin) *vis-à-vis* outsiders. The competitive position of insiders *vis-à-vis* other insiders, in a third market remains unchanged.

The lower part of Figure 1 focuses on the changes of the competitive position of R (the outsider) *vis-à-vis* the insiders. Depending on the source of competition, R's competitive position either deteriorates or improves moderately. Its competitive position *vis-à-vis* domestic manufacturers improves by a small margin. Relative to other insiders, the competitive position of R clearly deteriorates.

The wide-ranging program that constitutes EC92 causes an environmental shock requiring far reaching responses and adjustments at both the macro- and microeconomic levels.

At the macro level the apparatus of the state must be mobilized. Indeed the small outsider countries Austria, Sweden and Finland came to the conclusion that, following the completion of the European single market, they could no longer afford to stay outside. The governments of these countries negotiated accession agreements and became full members on January 1, 1995.

The governments of other countries that, for various reasons, cannot or will not join the European Union are seeking other types of agreements that would neutralize to some extent the negative effects of EC92. Israel, for example, is seeking to renegotiate its free trade area agreement with the European Union. The negotiations cover the important areas of public procurement and of research and development. If this effort is successful, the revised agreement should diminish the negative consequences of being an outsider country.

The ability to ameliorate the negative consequences of EC92 at the macroeconomic level depends primarily on the bargaining position of the country in question and on the attitude of the population towards closer political and economic relations with the European Union. The rejection of the proposed agreement on the European Economic Area by the citizens of Switzerland indicates that some countries are unwilling to accept the diminution of sovereignty that full membership in the European Union implies.

The focus of this study, however, is not on states but rather on business firms. In considering their response to EC92, firms enjoy much more freedom than the states in which they are headquartered. All Swedish firms became insiders when Sweden joined the European Union. However, even before Sweden joined the European Union, some individual firms choose to become insiders simply by establishing themselves within the European Union. Moreover, a firm can achieve insider status without moving its head office to an European Union country. To achieve insider status it is sufficient to establish a subsidiary in a country belonging to the European Union. It is hardly surprising that a large number of firms have chosen this option. The wish to achieve insider status seems indeed to have been the main motivation behind many FDI decisions by outsider firms in recent years. For example, in its Fourth Following Report, dealing with the effects of EC92 on the United States, the US International Trade Commission (1992) noted: "Another important factor in drawing direct investment to the EC has been the 1992 single-market program. Fear of being excluded from the EC market after the integration program is complete has apparently increased the willingness of US and Japanese companies to earmark funds for European projects". Similar views about the motivation behind increased FDI in the European Union by outsiders have been expressed by other writers (Ozawa 1992; Yannopoulous 1990; Rugman and Verbeke 1991). Balasubramanyam and Greenaway (1992), found evidence that Japanese FDI has increased as a consequence of the 1992 program. Dunning (1991) reported a marked increase in United States direct investment in all European Union countries towards 1992.

He noted that investment in the European Union in 1989 and 1990 accounted for nearly 50% of all United States foreign plant and equipment expenditure, as opposed to 38.8% in 1985.

The propensity of outsiders to invest in the European Union as well as the scope and actual mode of investment are influenced by several additional factors. Firm characteristics and the related product characteristics are expected to figure prominently among these factors. The relationship between these attributes and the response to EC92 is discussed in the following section.

III. Firm attributes, product attributes, and the response to EC92

Industrial firms produce outputs that can be conveniently divided into two broad groups: Schumpeter goods and Heckscher-Ohlin goods (Hirsch 1974; Hirsch and Meshulach 1991).[2] The distinction between Schumpeter and Heckscher-Ohlin goods is based on the attributes of the factors used in their manufacture. Some production factors are universal, others are firm-specific. Universal factors are available at the prevailing market price to all economic entities, regardless of whether they are owned by domestic or foreign firms. Examples include natural resources, unskilled and skilled labor, physical, financial and human capital, infrastructure, and the services provided by public institutions. Firm-specific factors are represented by the technical and managerial expertise and the experience embodied in its managers, engineers, skilled workers and other employees. It takes the form of codified and noncodified operating norms and policies as well as past investments in process engineering and in product research and development. An important attribute of firm-specific knowledge is that competitors can be effectively prevented from gaining access to it (Cantwell 1990).

Relating inputs to outputs, we note that Schumpeter goods contain a significant element of proprietary or firm-specific knowledge that imparts unique characteristics to the product. By contrast, Heckscher-Ohlin goods contain a relatively small element of proprietary knowledge and depend mostly on universal inputs. Employing the product life cycle framework,

---

[2] We use the term good rather than product so as to emphasize the distinction between goods and services, which is considered in some detail below.

we might refer to Schumpeter goods with new products belonging to the early phase of the cycle and Heckscher-Ohlin goods as belonging to the mature phase.

Associated with each good is a bundle of services that must be rendered to make it useful to customers. Though services, like goods, are outputs of a production process, they are distinguishable from goods by the following attributes: services are intangible, and cannot be inventoried; to render a service, the provider must interact with the user (Hirsch 1989).

In services, as in goods, we distinguish between universal services (Heckscher-Ohlin services) and firm-specific services (Schumpeter services). The distinction in this case depends on the source of the knowledge required to provide the service. Schumpeter services (instruction, installation, repairs, etc.) depend onproprietary knowledge originating with the manufacturer of the goods. These services can be provided by the good manufacturer or by organizations to whom the relevant knowledge was transferred (distributors, for example). Heckscher-Ohlin services (for example, finance, insurance and transportation) are usually provided by specialist firms. Specialization in this case relates to the nature of the service and only rarely to the characteristics of the service users.

Since firm-specific knowledge is relatively unimportant in Heckscher-Ohlin goods, we expect these goods to be mostly associated with Heckscher-Ohlin services. Schumpeter services are, on the other hand, more likely to be associated with Schumpeter goods. These characteristics influence the operating modes employed in the manufacture and distribution of goods and their associated services.

Having specified the attributes of Heckscher-Ohlin goods and Schumpeter goods industries, we are ready to examine the likely response to EC92 of outsider firms producing one of the two types of goods for European Union markets. EC92 is going to change the economics of forward market integration, as shown in the following examples.

Consider German and Israeli manufacturers of medical scanning equipment – a typical Schumpeter good, requiring intensive associated services such as instruction, installation, maintenance and repairs (all Schumpeter type services). The firms operate manufacturing plants in their respective home countries from which they ship their output to customers located throughout the European Union. Prior to EC92, these services could not be provided across national boundaries. Hence, the firms' customers had to be serviced by local facilities in the target markets. Since the number of installations in each country was considered too small to justify the establishment of distribution and service subsidiaries, the servicing was provided by local independent distributors.

Comparing the position of the two firms prior to EC92, note that they compete on more or less equal terms in the different European Union markets. The only exception is Germany, the local firm could use its manufacturing base to service its local customer.

Following EC92, the relative competitive position of the two firms changes radically, since European Union-based firms are able to export their services across national boundaries. Thus, the German firm can service all its European Union customers from any location inside the Union. The firm is able to transfer its servicing operations to the home facility, which it owns and controls. The home facility shares overhead with production, research and development, and other functions. To compete with the German firm on a similar basis in the European Union markets, the Israeli firm must engage in FDI in at least one market. Ceteris Paribus, its competitive position has deteriorated following EC92.

Next, consider again the effects of EC92 on the competitive position of the Israeli and Spanish plywood producers discussed previously. The elimination of intra-European Union border controls as a result of EC92 will give the Spanish insider a competitive edge over the Israeli competitor. The latter, however, is unlikely to suffer from additional disabilities due to EC92. Being a typical Heckscher-Ohlin good, whose characteristics and uses are well known, the marketing of plywood requires few firm-specific services dependent on the manufacturer. Consequently, warehousing and distribution, which are the most important associated services, can be easily handled by independent organizations. EC92 may encourage the establishment of regional distribution centers, these can be easily operated by organizations unrelated to the plywood manufacturers, given their Heckscher-Ohlin type characteristics. Consequently we expect less FDI in the plywood industry than in medical instruments.

Though the examples discussed above are highly specific, they suggest a general proposition: Schumpeter and Heckscher-Ohlin goods producers will tend to respond differently to the challenges of EC92. Ceteris Paribus, the former's propensity to engage in FDI in the European Union will be higher than the latter's. This proposition pertains particularly to what Dunning has termed market seeking FDI, that is, FDI intended to enhance or defend the market position of the investing firm in the target country (Dunning 1988; Stopford, Strange and Henley 1991) and is operationalized in the following section.

IV. Hypotheses

We have shown that FDI is likely to figure prominently among the steps taken by outsiders to counteract the negative challenges of EC92 and exploit the positive one. In this section we present a number of testable hypotheses derived from the theoretical analysis that predict the patterns of FDI flows in response to the realization of EC92. Next, the expected patterns are compared with actual FDI flows to determine the extent to which actual FDI patterns are consistent with expectations.

Response via increased FDI flows to EC92 may be expected to be particularly noticeable in economies that trade intensively with the European Union, such as the Israeli economy.

Israel is a small open economy, that is highly dependent on international transactions for its economic well-being. Exports plus imports reached 83% of its GNP in 1990. Its economic relations with the European Union are close. Since 1975 Israel has had a Free Trade Area Agreement with the European Union. Under the agreement, two-way trade in industrial goods (but excluding agricultural produce and food products) is tariff free and not subject to quota restrictions. Exports to the European Union accounted in 1991 for 36% of total exports, and imports from the European Union accounted for 48% of total imports.

The analysis in the preceding sections indicates that, despite the Free Trade Area Agreement between Israel and the European Union, the competitive position of Israeli firms is going to be adversely affected by EC92. To counteract these adverse effects, Israeli firms will tend, as noted above, to engage in market seeking FDI in the European Union. Following are a number of specific hypotheses derived from our analysis:

H1. **F(EU) pre-1987< F(EU) post-1987.**
> where:
> F = FDI by Israeli firms
> EU = European Union markets

Conditions of access by Israeli exporters to EC markets were specified in the 1975 Free Trade Area Agreement between the EC and Israel. The decision on EC92, taken in 1986 and ratified in 1987, constitutes the only major change in the conditions of access to EC markets. Hypothesis 1 states the expectation that Israeli firms would respond to EC92 by increasing FDI in the EU in order to reduce the adverse effects of EC92 by obtaining the status of insiders.

H2. **F(US) pre-1987 > F(EU) pre-1987**
where:
US = United States

H3. $\dfrac{\textbf{F(EU)}}{\textbf{F(US)}}$ **pre-1987** $<$ $\dfrac{\textbf{F(EU)}}{\textbf{F(US)}}$ **post-1987**

Comparisons between the United States and the European Union as target markets for Israeli FDI are appropriate since Israel has free trade area agreements with both. Market access conditions in the two areas are therefore similar. We contend that prior to 1987, FDI in the United States was preferred to FDI in the European Union because of high barriers to intra-European Union transactions (which EC92 seeks to remove). Adoption of the Single European Act in 1987 reduced the advantage of the United States in attracting FDI. Hypotheses 2 and 3 follow from the above. Hypothesis 2 states the expectation that prior to 1987 the propensity of Israeli firms to engage in FDI in the United States was higher than the propensity to invest in the European Union. Hypothesis 3 suggests that the relative attractiveness of the European Union as a target for FDI has increased after 1987, in anticipation of the realization of the EC92 program.

H4. **F (s) > F (h)**
where:
(s) = Schumpeter goods
(h) = Heckscher-Ohlin goods

Hypothesis 4 follows from our discussion regarding the characteristics of Heckscher-Ohlin and Schumpeter goods. Forward market integration (that is, direct distribution through organizations controlled by the good's producer) will be higher among Schumpeter goods than among Heckscher-Ohlin goods producers. This conclusion should carry over into the international arena, where we expect FDI to be more prevalent among Schumpeter goods than among Heckscher-Ohlin goods firms.

H5. **EU** $\dfrac{\textbf{F(s)}}{\textbf{F(h)}}$ **pre-1987** $<$ **EU** $\dfrac{\textbf{F(s)}}{\textbf{F(h)}}$ **post-1987**

Combining H1 and H4, we expect the ratio of FDI in Schumpeter goods to Heckscher-Ohlin goods to increase in anticipation of EC92. Specifically, we hypothesize that the post-1987 FDI ratio of the Schumpeter goods to Heckscher-Ohlin goods in the European Union will be higher than the pre-1987 ratio.

Before we discuss the patterns of FDI from Israel, a number of comments about the economy and the institutional arrangements governing FDI from Israel are in order.

Israel is one of the few market-oriented economies where outgoing FDI is subject to specific government approval. Consequently, the use of FDI among Israeli firms is a relatively new phenomenon. Figures presented a previously (Almor-Ellemers and Hirsch 1991) showed that the cumulative value of foreign investments represented less than USD 500 million by the end of 1984, or about 10% of industrial exports in that year. By comparison, Japan, whose FDI is also of relatively recent origin, had a cumulative FDI of USD 71,431 million in 1984, representing about 30% of that year's exports (Kojima 1990).

Cumulative FDI by Israeli companies tripled during the subsequent six years, reaching USD 1,563 million by December 1991. Growth of FDI has been very rapid since 1985. By comparison, growth in exports fluctuated around 10%, except for 1987, when exports increased by 17%.

Data concerning FDI by Israeli firms were provided by the Foreign Exchange Department of the Bank of Israel, which supervises foreign investments. Permission to invest abroad is, as a rule, granted to firms that can demonstrate that their investment will increase exports. FDI by Israeli firms can consequently be considered to be primarily motivated by market seeking, a motive that is consistent with the aforementioned hypothesis.

Two sets of figures were available to us – the number of investments (or rather of approvals) and their value. The decision of firms to engage in forward market integration is manifested by the number of foreign affiliates they control and not necessarily by the amount of money spent on their acquisition, which may vary between firms, industries, countries and functions. However, presenting the data in terms of value as well as number or affiliates gives a more complete picture, both data sets were therefore included.

Results

In this section hypothesized FDI flows are compared with the actual flows exhibited by all firms engaged in FDI prior to the end of 1991.[3] The computation of sampling errors and of significance levels is consequently unnecessary, and the extent of agreement between the expected and actual flows can be immediately deduced from the figures. Agreement between the direction of predicted and actual flows cannot, however, be interpreted as empirical confirmation of the theoretical discussion. This kind of interpretation is justified only if it can be shown that the FDI patterns are inconsistent with alternative theories. Since such a claim cannot be made on the basis of FDI flows from a single country, the following empirical analysis is offered as an example and not as an attempt to prove or disprove a theory.

Hypothesis 1 concerns investments in the European Union before and after 1987.

H1.   **F(EU) pre-1987< F(EU) post-1987.**

FDI for two time periods': 1984-1987 and 1988-1991, is shown in Table 1. The number of Israeli investments in the Union was 74 between 1984 and 1987 and 387 between 1988 and 1991, which represents an increase of over 500%. The value of Israeli FDI in the European Union increased from USD 94 million between 1984 and 1987 to USD 262 million between 1988 and 1991. This pattern is consistent with the expectation that post-EC92 FDI flows would exceed pre-European Union 92 flows.

H2.   **F(US) pre-1987 > F(EU) pre-1987**

FDI in the United States[4] was expected to be larger than that in the European Union before 1987 due to the absence of barriers within the United

---

[3] The FDI data obtained pertain to all approvals granted by the Bank of Israel, aggregated by country of destination and by industry. Approvals of FDI do not necessarily correspond to FDI actually taking place in a given year. Some investments are inevitably delayed and others are canceled. We believe, however, that the figures provided by the Bank of Israel represent a reasonable proxy for FDI undertaken by Israeli firms in the period under consideration.

[4] The Bank of Israel would not provide us with data for FDI in the United States only, and supplied data on North America (United States and Canada) instead. As FDI is compared to exports in the same geographical area, we defined exports in terms of North America as well. Although this is not completely accurate, the deviation is quite small since Canada accounted for less than 3% of Israel's exports.

Table 1. FDI and exports to the United States and European Community, 1984-
1987 and 1988-1991.

Cumulative figures for each time period		1984-1987	1988-1991	1984-1991
Raw data:				
FDI number of cases	EC	74	387	461
	US	107	299	406
FDI (millions of USD)	EC	94	262	356
	US	77	465	542
Exports (millions of USD)	EC	6,134	11,383	17,517
	US	4,583	8,888	13,471
Normalized Figures:				
FDI (EC) cases		1.20	3.40	2.60
FDI (EC) USD		1.50	2.30	2.00
FDI (US) cases		2.30	3.40	3.00
FDI (US) USD		1.70	5.20	4.00
FDI (EC)/FDI (US) cases		0.69	1.29	1.14
FDI (EC)/FDI (US) USD		1.22	0.56	0.66

Sources: **FDI** – figures provided by the Bank of Israel.
Exports – Central Bureau of Statistics, Statistical Abstract of Israel,
Jerusalem, Government Printing Office, various years

States. To test the hypothesis, it is necessary to neutralize the effect of the absolute size of the two markets. Reasoning that exports represent in some sense the relevant market potential of the United States and the Union, we divided FDI by the cumulative exports for each time period to the two markets.

First, we compared the number of investments per USD 100 million of exports. Before 1987 there were 1.20 cases of FDI per USD 100 million of exports to the Union. The Comparable figures in the United States before 1987 were 2.30. These results are consistent with expectations derived from hypothesis 2. Comparisons in dollar terms show the same patterns. Investments in the pre-87 Union markets represented USD 1.50 per USD 100 of export. Investment in the pre 87 United States market represents USD 1.70 per USD 100 of export. Actual FDI patters are consistent with expected patterns in terms of value as well as number of investments.

H3. $$\frac{F(EU)}{F(US)} \text{ pre-1987} < \frac{F(EU)}{F(US)} \text{ post-1987}$$

Combining hypotheses 1 and 2, it is expected that FDI in the Union would increase at a higher rate than in the United States in anticipation of EC92.

The figures presented in Table 1 are only partially consistent with the expectations. When FDI is measure by the number of investment approvals, the Union/United States ratio increases from 0.69 (74/107) to 1.29 (387/299), that corresponds with our hypothesis. In value terms, however, the Union/United States ratio decreases from 1.22 (94 / 77) to 0.56 (262 / 465) between the two periods. Judged by this measure, hypothesis 3 must be rejected.

In our view, the number of FDI projects rather than their absolute value is the appropriate unit of analysis in the present context, as the following example shows. Consider FDI by six firms: five invest USD 100,000 in the Union, and the remaining firm invests USD 1,000,000 dollars in the United States. Judged by the value criterion, FDI in the United States exceeds FDI in the Union by a factor of 2 to 1. Judged by the criterion of the number of FDI projects, FDI in the Union exceeds FDI in the United States by a factor of 5 to 1. The number criterion is superior as long as each FDI project enables the investing firm to achieve insider status. This

Table 2. R&D Expenditure, Percentage of Technical Personnel and Employment Cost by Industry.

Industry	R&D as % of turnover	Technical personnel *	Employment cost **
Heckscher-Ohlin-Industry:			
Food & beverages	0.2	4.0	15.8
Textile & clothing	0.1	4.3	11.5
Plastic & Rubber	0.7	9.8	15.4
Metal products	0.4	10.5	21.5
Schumpeter-Industry:			
Chemicals	1.7	16.6	29.3
Electric & Electronics	6.4	37.4	30.7
Average for Industry (not including diamonds):	**1.6**	**13.7**	**20.9**

Source: Ben Aharon, N. 7 Toren, B. *A data base for minor branches of industry, Research Report No. 16.* Jerusalem: Jerusalem Institute for Israel Studies, 1993.
*   Technical personnel (engineers, academics, technicians) employed in industry as percentage of overall employees.
**   Employment cost in thousands of USD per year.

indeed is the case since foreign subsidiaries are considered Union firms under the rules of EC92. A sales and servicing subsidiary operating in any Union market is thus able to distribute and service imported goods in all Union markets, regardless of the amount of money it invests.

Hypotheses 4 and 5 concern the different propensity of Heckscher-Ohlin and Schumpeterian manufacturers to engage in FDI. The dividing line between Schumpeterian and Heckscher-Ohlin export industries was as follows. In Schumpeter industries, the R&D-to-sales ratio is higher than 1.5%, the ratio of skilled employees exceeds 15% and average annual employment costs exceed USD 25,000. In Heckscher-Ohlin industries all three measures have lower values. Thus, chemicals, electrical and electronic products are classified as Schumpeter goods industries, whereas food and beverages, textiles and clothing, plastics and rubber and metal products are classified as Heckscher-Ohlin goods industries.

Hypothesis 4 posits that FDI in Schumpeter goods industries is higher than in Heckscher-Ohlin goods industries.

H4.   **F (s) > F (h)**

Table 3 presents figures concerning the relation between FDI (cumulative between 1984 and 1991) and exports (for the year 1989)[5] for both Heckscher-Ohlin goods and Schumpeter goods. The figures are consistent with the expectation that the propensity of Schumpeter firms to engage in FDI is higher than that of Heckscher-Ohlin firms. In absolute terms, Schumpeter goods manufacturers made 455 foreign investments costing USD 586 million, compared with 131 foreign investments costing USD 68 million by Heckscher-Ohlin goods manufacturers. The same pattern is evident in normalized terms (investments over exports).

Hypothesis 5 concerns FDI by Schumpeter and Heckscher-Ohlin goods manufacturers in the Union only, before and after 1987.

H5. EU $\dfrac{\text{F(s)}}{\text{F(h)}}$ pre-1987 $<$ $\dfrac{\text{EUF(s)}}{\text{F(h)}}$ post-1987

[5] Although it would be more accurate to compare FDI to export data weighted over time, such data were not available. The year 1989 was chosen as a basis for normalizing FDI figures for technical reasons which included a division in that year between electrical products (Heckscher-Ohlin goods) and electronics (Schumpeter goods), usually lumped together by Israel's Central Bureau of Statistics. The FDI and export figures are for manufacturing industries only. Service industries and nonclassified investments were not included.

Table 3. FDI by Schumpeter-good and Heckscher-Ohlin-good firms, 1984-1991.

	Heckscher-Ohlin-Goods	Schumpeter-goods
FDI (number of cases)	131	455
FDI (millions of USD) *	68	586
Exports **	2,569	2,772
Normalized figures:		
FDI (cases) ***	5.1	16.4
FDI (millions of USD) ***	2.6	21.1

Sources: See Table 1
*   Cumulative between 1984 and 1991
**   Exports in millions of USD in 1989
***   Multiplied by 100 and divided by exports

The data obtained from the Bank of Israel do not allow for a simultaneous comparison of FDI by industrial sector between regions and across time periods. Hypothesis 5 was therefore tested on data obtained from a sample of 84 leading firms engaged in trade and FDI in the European Union (Almor-Ellemers 1993). The data presented in Table 4 pertain to wholly owned subsidiaries only.

The investments were divided into three time periods: 1960-1980, 1981-1987, 1988-1991. The FDI ratio of Schumpeter to Heckscher-Ohlin goods industries increased from 1.07 in the first time period to 2.00 in the second period and to 3.00 in the third. Schumpeter goods firms, compared with Heckscher-Ohlin goods firms, set up three times as many subsidiaries in the Union between 1988 and 1991. The figures are consistent with the expectation that FDI patterns have been influenced by EC92.

Conclusions

By establishing affiliates in the European Union, outsider firms can acquire the status of insiders which, in theory at least, have the same rights and obligations as firms owned by Union nationals. Admittedly, the experience of Japanese automotive and computer firms indicates that the right of non-Union firms to insider status is not automatically guaranteed. It is

Table 4. Number of wholly owned subsidiaries in the EC set up by 84 exporting firms by time period and type of goods.

	1960-1980	1981-1987	1988-1991	Total
Heckscher-Ohlin-goods	14	8	6	28
Schumpeter-goods	15	16	18	49
Total	29	24	24	77
Schumpeter-goods/ Heckscher-Ohlin-goods	1.07	2.00	3.00	1.75

Source: Almor-Ellemers (1993).

nevertheless likely that the principle of national treatment will, on the whole, be observed in the Union, provided non-Europeans, on their part, demonstrate their adherence to the idea of reciprocity.

The findings reported in this chapter support our hypotheses on the whole. Since these findings are based on the entire population of Israeli firms, there can be no doubt about their statistical significance. It should, however, be remembered that the FDI patterns exhibited by Israeli firms may well be influenced by the restrictions imposed on capital exports and by other country-specific conditions. It is possible that patterns of behavior in other countriesmay be different.

Bearing these caveats in mind, it is probably safe to generalize from our findings concerning the response of different outsider groups to EC92. These findings, underpinned by the theoretical analysis, are:

1. When engaging in market seeking FDI, firms prefer to establish affiliates in large non-fragmented markets. This preference has two manifestations: FDI in the unified United States market has been larger than in the fragmented European Union. At the same time outsider firms have been anticipating the completion of the single market and have been increasing their FDI in Europe at a higher rate than in the United States since 1988.

2. The propensity of Schumpeter goods manufacturers to engage in FDI has been higher than that of Heckscher-Ohlin goods manufacturers. Moreover, the rate of investment in the European Union by Schumpeter-

ian firms in comparison with that of Heckscher-Ohlin firms has been increasing in recent years in an apparent response to the approaching completion date of the European single market.

References

Almor, T. and S. Hirsch (1995): Outsiders' Response to Europe 1992: Theoretical Considerations and Empirical Evidence. *Journal of International Business Studies 26*: 223-237.

Almor-Ellemers, T. (1993): *International strategic alliances: A Means to Cope with a Changing Environment – 1992: Israel and a Single European Market.* Unpublished doctoral dissertation. Tel Aviv University.

Almor-Ellemers, T. and S. Hirsch. (1991): *Patterns of Foreign Direct Investment: Israel, a Small Country Situated in between Trading Blocks. Business and Economic Studies on European Integration.* Copenhagen. Institute of International Economics and Management, Copenhagen Business School, WP 9-91.

Baldwin, R. (1989):.The growth effects of 1992. *Economic Policy* October: 248-281.

Balasubramanyam, U. N. and D. Greenaway (1992): Economic Integration and Foreign Direct Investment: Japanese Investment in the EC. *Journal of Common Market Studies* 30: 175-193.

Cantwell, J. (1990): *The technological competence theory of international production and its implications. Discussion Papers in International Investment and Business Studies.* 149. (mimeo) Readsig. University of Reading Department of Economics.

Cecchini, P., M. Catinat and A. Jacquemin (1988): *1992: The European Challenge – The Benefits of a Single Market.* London: Wildwood House.

Commission of the European Communities (1988): *The Economics of 1992 – An Assessment of the Potential Economic Effects of Completing the Internal Market of the EC.*

Dunning, J.H. (1988). The Eclectic Paradigm of International Production: A Restatement and some Possible Extensions. *Journal of International Business Studies* 19: 1-31.

Dunning, J. H. (1991): *European integration and Transatlantic Foreign Direct Investment: The Record Assessed. Business and Economic Studies on European Integration.* Copenhagen. Institute of International Economics and Management, Copenhagen Business School, WP 3/91.

Hirsch, S. (1974): Hypotheses regarding Trade Between Developing and Industrial Countries. In H Giersch (ed.) *The International Division of Labour Problems and Perspectives.* Kiel: Kiel Institute of World Economics.

Hirsch, S. (1989): Services and Service Intensity in International Trade. *Weltwirtschafliches Archiv* 125: 45-60.

Hirsch, S. (1990): *Nineteen Ninety Two: How Will Outsiders Be Affected?* Tel Aviv: The Israel Institute of Business Research, Tel Aviv University, WP 66/90.

Hirsch, S. and A. Meshulach. (1991): Towards a Unified Theory of Internationalization. In H Vestergaard (ed.) *An Enlarged Europe in the Global Economy vol. 1 577-601.* Copenhagen: European International Business Association (EIBA): 577-601.

Kojima, K. (1990): *Japanese Direct Investment Abroad.* Tokyo: International Christian University.

Meade, J. E. (1955): The Theory of Customs Unions, Amsterdam: North Holland. The *DeVries Lectures,* Vol. 1.

Ozawa, T. (1992): Cross-investment between Japan and the EC: Income Similarity, Product Variation, and Economies of Scope. In J Cantwell (ed.) *Multinational Investment in Modern Europe: Strategic Interaction in the Integrated Community.* Cheltenham: Edward Elgar Publishing.

Rugman, A. M. and S. A. Verbeke. (1991): Competitive strategies for non-European firms. In B. Burgenmeier and J. L. Mucchielli (eds.) *Multinationals and Europe 1992.* London: Routledge.

Stopford, J., S. Strange, and J. S. Henley (1991): *Rival States, Rival Firms; Competition for World Market Shares.* Cambridge: Cambridge University Press.

Tovias, A. (1990): The Impact of Liberalizing Government Procurement Policies of Individual EC Countries on Trade with Non-Members. *Weltwirtschaftliches Archiv* 126: 723-736.

United States International Trade Commission. (1992): *The Effects of Greater Economic Integration within the European Community on the United States: Fourth Following Report.* Washington, DC: US International Trade Commission.

Viner, J. (1950): *The Customs Union Issue,* New York Carnegie Endowment for International Peace, London: Stevens.

Yannopoulous, G. (1990): Foreign Direct Investment and European Integration: Evidence from the Formative Years of the European Community. *Journal of Common Market Studies* 28: 235-259.

Chapter 2:
The Response of
Small Outsider Countries
to the EC 1992 Program

Some Stylized Facts

Lars Oxelheim and Robert Gärtner

During the 1980s, corporate managers had to face many major changes in structural and institutional prerequisites. Deregulation on a global scale and a general dismantling of capital controls, coupled with substantial improvement in information technologies, facilitated a dramatic increase in foreign direct investment (FDI).[6]

As can be seen from Table 5, worldwide FDI outflows and outward stock increased dramatically during the latter half of the 1980s. Furthermore, exports increased significantly slower than outward FDI flows.[7] The importance of FDI and FDI-related trade for the world economy increased during the 1980s and beginning of the 1990s, as is shown in Table 6.

Small countries outside the European Union may have reacted to the EC 1992 program in two ways: it may have been regarded by investors as providing new investment opportunities or as signaling a future Fortress Europe with trade discriminating against companies located in non-member countries. Hence, from a welfare point of view, the EC 1992 program may have been investment creating and/or investment diverting in scope (Sweeney 1993).[8] As shown in Figures 2-6, a dramatic upswing in out-

---

[6] For a definition and general statistical problems encountered in measuring FDI, see Appendix I.

[7] The reason could be that, as pointed out by Markusen (1994), most FDI seems to be "horizontal", in that the major part of the output of foreign affiliates is sold in the host country.

[8] The issue of investment creation and investment diversion effects of the EC 1992 Program has also been discussed in Baldwin, Forslid and Haaland (1994), suggesting that the EC 1992 Program has been investment diverting in EFTA countries, and investment-creating in EU countries.

Table 5. Worldwide FDI and selected economic indicators, for 1992, and growth rates for 1981-1985, 1986-1990, 1991 and 1992 (billions of USD and percentage.

Indicator	Value at current prices	Annual growth rate (%)			
	1992	1982-1985 [a]	1986-1990 [a]	1991	1992
FDI outflows	171	3.0	24	-17	-11
FDI outward stock	2,125[b]	5.0	11	10	6
Sales of foreign affiliates of TNCs[c]	4,800[d]	2.0[e]	15	-13	-
Current gross domestic product at factor cost	23,300	2.0	9	4	5
Gross domestic investment	5,120	0.4	10	4	5
Exports of goods and non-factor services	, 4,500[d]	-0.2	13	3	-
Royalty and fees receipts	37	0.1	19	8	5

[a] Compounded growth rate estimates, based on a semi-logarithmic regression equation.
[b] 1993.
[c] Estimated by exptrapolating the worldwide sales of foreign affiliates of TNCs from Germany, Japan and the United States on the basis of the relative importance of these countries in worldwide outward FDI stock.
[d] 1991.
[e] 1982-1985.
Source: UNCTAD, Division on Transnational Corporations and Investment, *World Investment Report 1994: Transnational Corporations, Employment and the Workplace* (United Nations publications, Sales No. E.94.II.A. 14).

ward FDI came about for some outsider countries[9] in 1987-1988. The magnitude and timing of the upturn provides an argument for causality, in that companies of outsider countries were forced to make decisions in response to the approval of the Single Act. The immediate aggregate response reflects the relatively high dependence on the Union market and a high number of foot-loose multinationals. The true magnitude of this policy change may be seen by the extent that the outsider countries have adopted counteracting policies. As discussed by Oxelheim (1993), the

[9] Our sample of small outsider countries consists of the largest EFTA countries (Austria, Finland, Norway, Sweden and Switzerland). In addition to these, Israel was included as being a country with a large share of trade with the European Union (see Appendix II). Since figures on Swiss outward FDI were not obtainable, we had to exclude Switzerland from all figures except Figures 7-11.

Table 6. The role of FDI in world economic activity, 1913, 1960, 1975, 1980, 1985 and 1991 (Percentages).

Item	1913	1960	1975	1980	1985	1991
World FDI stock as a share of world output	9.0 [a]	4.4	4.5	4.8	6.4	8.5
World FDI inflows as a share of world output	-	0.3	0.3	0.5	0.5	0.7
World FDI inflows as a share of world gross fixed capital formation	-	1.1	1.4	2.0	1.8	3.5
World sales of foreign affiliates as a share of world exports	-	84 [b]	97 [c]	99 [d]	99 [d]	122

[a] Estimate.
[b] 1967 based on United States figures.
[c] Based on United States and Japanese figures.
[d] 1982 based on German, Japanese and United States data.
Source: UNCTAD, Division on Transnational Corporations and Investment, *World Investment Report 1994: Transnational Corporations, Employment and the Workplace* (United Nations publication, Sales No. E.94.II.A.14).

Figure 2. Flows of total Austrian outward FDI and FDI to the EC 1984-1991: Net investment, million MATS, 1984 prices.

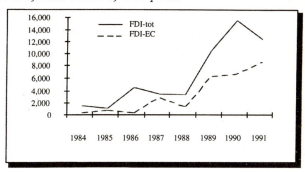

Source: Based on data from EFTA, *Occ. Paper and OECD, Survey Austria.*

lowering of corporate taxes, provision of subsidies, looser interpretation of international agreements (for example, social dumping) etc. are all elements of such counteracting policies and part of a global race for FDI.

The industrialized countries are not only responsible for most outward direct investment, they also constitute the major recipients of FDI. Moreover, there is a great deal of two-way FDI flows between pairs of industrialized countries (Markusen 1994). Thus, the bulk of the increase in for-

Figure 3. Flows of total Finnish outward FDI and FDI to the EC 1984-1991: annual net investment, millions of FIM, 1984 prices.

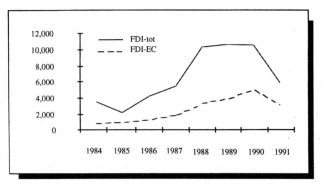

Source: Based on data from ETLA, *database.*

eign direct investment was undertaken by countries of similar per capita incomes and similar factor endowments. However, as can be seen from Figures 7-11, outward FDI from a number of OECD countries outside the Union has in general been greater than inward FDI to these countries. Furthermore, the gap between outward and inward FDI widened following the years 1987-1988.

Where did the investments go? According to Dunning's OLI paradigm, multinationals tend to make investments in countries where they can enjoy an ownership advantage ('O') vis-à-vis firms of other nationalities

Figure 4. Flows of total Israeli outward FDI and FDI to the EC 1985-1991: annual net investment, million USD, 1985 prices.

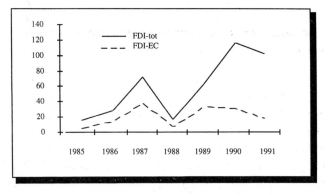

Source: Based on data from the Bank of Israel, *database.*

Figure 5. Flows of total Norwegian outward FDI and FDI to the EC 1984-1991: annual net investment, million NOK, 1984 prices.

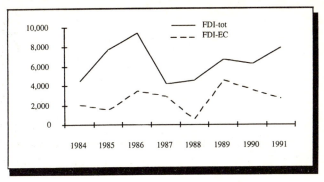

Source: Based on data from the Central Bank of Norway, *database*.

(Dunning 1993). Mainly, this concerns advantages unique to the company and arising from the possession of a superior production process, capital, personnel, or more intangible assets such as patents, trademarks or a reputation for quality. The 'L' stands for location advantage, and refers to advantages arising from access to cheap labor and other factor endowments, avoidance of tariffs and quotas, and other policy-induced market imperfections. The third item in Dunning's paradigm is internalization advantages ('I'), and refers to advantages that make it more appealing for the multinational corporation to set up a production plant abroad rather than just licensing a local company to produce the product or use the pro-

Figure 6. Flows of total Swedish outward FDI and FDI to the EC 1984-1991: annual net investment, million SEK, 1984 prices.

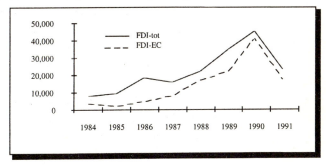

Source: Based on data from the Central Bank of Sweden, *database*.

Figure 7. Outward less inward Austrian FDI as a percentage of GDP 1982 - 1992.

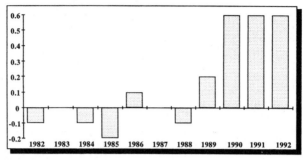

Source: OECD/DAF - Based on official national statistics from the balance of payments, *database.*

duction process. Examples of such advantages of hierarchical control could be avoidance of costs associated with moral hazards and adverse selection, and search and negotiation (circumvention of market failures), or the possibility of engaging in predatory pricing, cross-subsidization, transfer pricing etc. (exploitation of market failures). Hence, foreign production, as opposed to mere export or licensing agreements, will be undertaken by companies with a globalization strategy that have identified the different market failures and have found it to be in their best interest to make use of and add value to their 'O' advantages in a foreign location rather than to sell them.

FDI is generally said to be undertaken for five reasons (Behrman 1972 referred to in Dunning 1993): the company may be (i) a natural resource seeker, (ii) a market seeker, (iii) an efficiency seeker, (iv) a strategic asset or capability seeker or, more probably, (v) a combination of the above. In addition to these, the company may involve itself in FDI to escape restrictive legislation by home governments (escape investments); to support or substitute exports and other activities of the rest of the company (support investments); or in anticipation of future capital appreciation or income gain (passive investments). The natural resource seeker invests abroad to exploit location-bound resources, such as minerals and agricultural products; inexpensive and well educated labor; and technological capabilities, managerial and organizational skills, marketing expertise, etc. A market seeker invests abroad to sustain or protect existing markets as well as to exploit and promote new markets. This includes foreign investment undertaken in order to pursue a globalization and marketing strategy,

Figure 8. Outward less inward Finnish FDI as a percentage of GDP, 1982-1992.

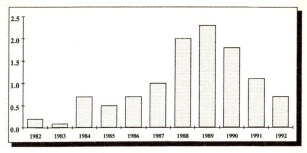

Source: OECD/DAF - Based on official national statistics from the balance of payments, *database.*

Figure 9. Outward less inward Norwegian FDI as a percentage of GDP, 1982-1992.

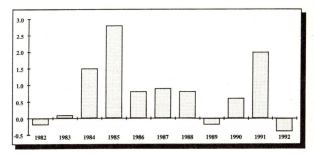

Source: OECD/DAF - Based on official national statistics from the balance of payments, *database.*

Figure 10. Outward less inward Swedish FDI as a percentage of GDP 1982-1992.

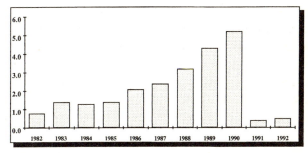

Source: OECD/DAF - Based on official national statistics from the balance of payments, *database.*

Figure 11. Outward less inward Swiss FDI as a percentage of GDP 1983-1991.

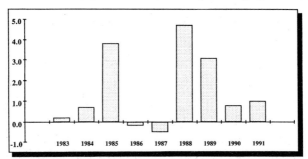

Source: OECD/DAF - Based on official national statistics from the balance of payments, *database.*

as well as investment opportunities created by host-country policies or investment prompted by (the perceived threat of) higher trade barriers implemented by the host-country authorities. Efficiency-seeking FDI is aimed at exploiting differences in the availability and costs of factor endowments among different countries or to take advantage of economies of scale and scope, risk diversification and differences in consumer demand. Finally, the strategic asset seeker may be engaged in FDI to pursue long-term strategies, such as maintaining international competitiveness, or to establish a competitive presence in unpenetrated markets.

Figures 2-6 illustrate outward FDI directed to the Union for some outsider countries. For Sweden, almost the entire increase in total FDI is explained by FDI in the Union (Figure 6), whereas the pattern is less clear-cut for other countries in the study. The large upswing in total outward Norwegian FDI during 1984-1986, as exhibited in Figure 5, was the result of non-access to an international shipping register. This non-access resulted in a major outflagging of ships, which was registered as outward FDI. In the case of Finland, we can see that the major increase in FDI was not directed to the Union. Indirectly, however, it was related to the EC 1992 program in that Finnish companies chose to use Sweden as an intermediate station on their way to the Union market[10] (Figure 3). The Israeli foreign investment pattern reflects domestic policy changes. In 1988, the

---

[10] During the period 1986 to 1990, Finnish companies were the most important investors in Sweden.

foreign reserves were so low that the Bank of Israel hardly enabled companies to invest outside Israel. However, in 1990, the Israeli policy regarding FDI became more flexible, implying a large increase in outward FDI. The upswing in FDI in 1990-1991, which was not directed towards the Union, is explained by two large investments – one in Africa and one in Southeast Asia (Figure 4). Finally, the increase in Austrian outward FDI between 1989 and 1990, which is not accounted for by FDI to the Union, can be attributed to a large extent to investment in central and eastern European countries. For instance, in 1989, the FDI stock in Hungary was MATS 660, while in 1990 it leaped to MATS 3,389. There are a few other explanations, such as large acquisitions in EFTA countries and one large investment in Australia. Moreover, the Austrian figures contain some technical problems in that the Austrian regional figures for 1984-1988 exclude banks, whereas the total figures include banks. FDI for the last quarter in 1991 has been estimated. Together, these data problems imply a need to interpret the Austrian flows with a certain degree of caution (Figure 2). However, even after having considered all data problems, the impression of the increased importance of the Union market following the presentation of the EC 1992 Program still remains for all the countries in the study.

Although the policy stance taken by the Union authorities could be seen as either investment -creating or investment-diverting in scope, many companies of the outsider countries seem to have perceived the policy change more as the threat of being excluded from the internal market than as an opportunity. Capturing a combination of market-seeking and strategic-asset seeking investment, the typical decision matrix of a company located in a non-Union country may have looked like the example in Table 7. The fictitious figures in the matrix are aimed at illustrating the relatively small extra profits earned from production at home as compared with the gigantic losses in the case of Fortress Europe. This means that even if there is a very small joint probability of non-membership and Fortress Europe (p_1), expected profits from production at home can be expected to be generally inferior to those from production located in the Union. In order to maintain long-term international competitiveness as well as to circumvent any higher barriers of trade, companies will locate production in the Union, even though it would be more profitable to produce at home for all other Union-membership scenarios. Hence, regardless of whether the policies adopted by the Union actually were investment-diverting in scope, or just perceived as such, they may have prompt-

Table 7. Decision matrix of companies located in non-European Union countries: an example.

		Becoming a member	Non-member	
			Fortress Europe	Non-Fortress Europe
	Probability	$1-p_1-p_2$	p_1	p_2
Decision	Production at home	100	-200	90
	Production in the Union	80	80	80

Note: In this simplified example, fictitious profits for different combinations of decision and Union membership scenario are given. Assuming for simplicity that the three outcomes in the table are equally probable, production at home gives an expected loss of 3.3 as compated to a profit of 80 for production inside the Union. Using expected profits as decision criterion, the company will produce in the Union, except when p_1 is zero or very small.

ed companies to increase the volume of investment within the Union.[11] Competing explanations to increased FDI inside the Union (for example, the trend for companies to adopt more global strategies, the need to attain a more competitive position before the completion of the internal market and the set of traditional investment-creating arguments) may add some explanatory value but may, according to interview studies (Braunerhjelm 1990) and official corporate statements from the contemporary debate, be seen as being inferior to the fear of Fortress Europe as the triggering factor.[12]

The magnitude of the response to the EC 1992 program and its investment-diverting content may differ across countries when studied at an aggregated level. Hence, the magnitude may vary depending on how much is at stake in the case of Fortress Europe, that is, depending on the relative importance of the Union market in the international trade of a particular country. In a global perspective, two major trading blocks may be identified relevant to the issue of this study: the Union and the United States markets. In Figures 12 through 16, cumulative FDI flows to these blocks are plotted. With the exception of Finland, we find that up until

[11] As long as the investors assign the probability p_1 a non-zero value, the EC 1992 program is to some extent investment-diverting.

[12] About the fear of exclusion as being the major cause for inflows of investments from outsider companies, see: Yamawaki (1990), Yannopoulous (1990, 1992), Ozawa (1992), Rugman and Verbeke (1991), and the US International Trade Commission (1992).

Figure 12. Austrian cumulative outward FDI to the European Community and the United States 1984-1991: net investment, million ATS, 1984 prices.

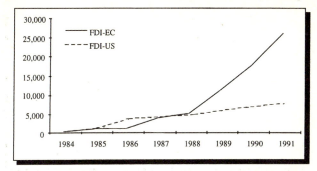

Source: Based on data from EFTA, *Occ. Paper* and OECD, *Survey Austria.*

Figure 13. Finnish cumulative outward FDI to the European Community and the United States 1984-1991: net investment, millions of FIM, 1984 prices.

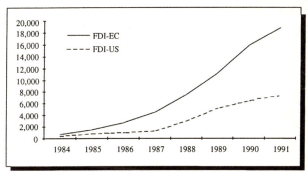

Source: Based on data from ETLA, *database*

1987-1988, the cumulative flows of FDI to the Union and the United States were more or less the same. Around 1987-1988, however, there is a clear break in the pattern for Austria, Norway, Sweden and (to some extent) Finland.[13] Contrary to this development, the Israeli cumulative FDI flows into the Union reveal no similar reaction. As shown by the export figures of Israel (see Appendix II), Israel's exports are, roughly, divided equally between the United States, the Union and the rest of the world – whereas the bulk of the exports from Austria, Finland, Norway

---

[13] Finland's reaction may have been smothered by the strong trade relations with the Soviet Union.

Figure 14. Israeli cumulative outward FDI to the European Community and the United States, 1985-1991: net investment, millions of USD, 1985 prices.

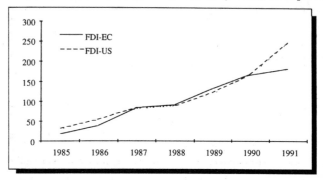

Source: Based on data from the Bank of Israel, *Database.* Data about FDI for the United States includes Canada.

Figure 15. Norwegian cumulative outward FDI to the European Community and the United States, 1984-1991: net investment, millions of NOK, 1984 prices.

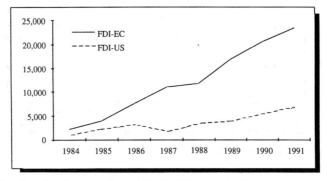

Source: Based on data from the Central Bank of Norway, *database*

and Sweden goes to the Union. Also, the physical, as well as the sociocultural proximity to the Union is closer for Austria, Finland, Norway and Sweden than for Israel. Around 1990, Israeli FDI flows into the United States clearly surpassed those into the Union. Due to the sociocultural proximity of Israel to the United States, this reaction may partly be attributed the North American Free Trade Area (NAFTA) discussions, which at that time entered a more concrete stage.

When it comes to the structure of outsider response, we may hypothe-

Figure 16. Swedish cumulative outward FDI to the European Community and the United States, 1984-1991: net investment, millions of SEK, 1984 prices.

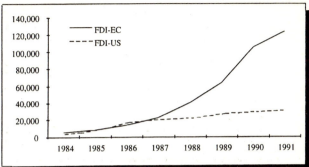

Source: Based on data from the Central Bank of Sweden, *database*

size that Union policies will influence different industries in small outsider countries in certain ways. The responsiveness to change in Union policy should be higher and faster in knowledge-intensive industries,[14] since they depend less upon comparative advantages arising from access to specific natural resources, and more on closeness to markets and networks and the upgrading of knowledge, than do less knowledge-intensive industries.[15] Being bound by high and infrequent investments in large-scale production facilities, Heckscher-Ohlin industries should then react more slowly to any change in market conditions. Thus, Schumpeter industry companies will be able to pull up stakes and relocate production elsewhere more readily than Heckscher-Ohlin industry companies. In our original sample (for companies of the only two small outsider countries for which data in this respect is available) the Schumpeter industry FDI flows in the post-1987 period were somewhat greater than those of the pre-1987 period. The Schumpeter industries in both Finland and Sweden seem to have reacted already to the presentation of the European Commission's White Paper of 1985 concerning the creation of the internal market, whereas the Heckscher-Ohlin industries' reaction came as late as in 1989-1990 in Fin-

[14] Hereafter called Schumpeter industries, encompassing industries belonging to ISIC groups 35 and 38. For further discussion, see Chapter 4.
[15] Hereafter called Heckscher-Ohlin industries, involving all manufacturing industries except ISIC 35 and 38. For further discussion, see Chapter 4.

Figure 17. Finnish cumulative outward FDI in Schumpeter- and Heckscher-Ohlin-industries, 1984-1991: net investment in manufacturing industries, millions of FIM, 1984 prices.

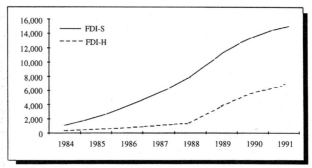

Source: Based on data from Koivisto (1993), and ETLA, *database.*

Figure 18. Swedish cumulative outward FDI in Schumpeter- and Heckscher-Ohlin-industries, 1984-1991: net investment in manufacturing industries, millions of SEK, 1984 prices.

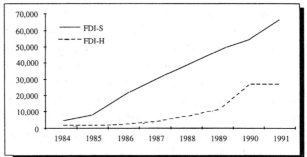

Source: Based on data from Central Bank of Sweden, *database.*

land and 1990 in Sweden (see Figures 17 and 18). However, the dramatic increase in outward FDI from Swedish Heckscher-Ohlin industries in 1990 was largely the result of just two large foreign acquisitions by the Swedish paper and pulp companies Stora and SCA, which acquired Feldmühle and Reedpack, respectively. For an in-depth discussion about Swedish Schumpeter and Heckscher-Ohlin industry FDI flows, see Chapter 4.

Conclusions

Worldwide FDI increased dramatically during the 1980s, the major part taking place between industrialized countries. The upswing was promoted by a global wave of deregulation, improvement in information technologies and regionalization. However, the gap between outward and inward FDI of a number of small non-Union countries shows that these countries were not major recipients of FDI. The timing and magnitude of the surge in outward FDI to the Union from these non-Union countries make it seem likely that the increase was a response by companies of these countries to changes in the policies of the Union authorities. These policies may have been perceived by companies in outsider countries either as opening up new profit opportunities, or as being a threat of a unified market not accessible to companies of non-member countries. Roughly at the time of the approval of the EC 1992 program, cumulative flows of FDI to the Union from most of the outsiders clearly overtook those to the United States. It seems that companies of outsider countries found it more important to make direct investments in the Union than in the United States market. As measured by shares of exports, the outsiders' stakes in the Union were significantly higher than in the United States. Hence, we subscribe to a view of causality between the creation of the EC 1992 program and outward direct investment in the Union from small outsider countries.

The character of the immediate reaction displayed by some outsiders in terms of outward FDI seems to support the argument that the EC 1992 program was perceived by companies in these countries as a threat rather than as an opportunity. Interview studies and statements made in the current debate further promote the argument that the EC 1992 program was perceived as investment-diverting by companies from non-member countries. Moreover, a response to the investment-creating parts of Union policies would probably have meant a longer time lag between the investment-triggering event and the actual investment.

Appendix I

Definitions of FDI and Statistical Problems

A direct investment implies a permanent relationship between the investor and the object of investment. According to the IMF (1993) definition of a foreign direct investment, the aim is to "acquire a lasting interest in an enterprise operating in an economy other than that of the investor, the investor's purpose being to have an effective voice in the management of the enterprise". The criterion "to have an effective voice" means a minimum 10% ownership in the invested object. FDI for all countries involved in the study, as exhibited in the figures, is defined according to this definition.

Although the countries in our sample all apply the same basic definition of FDI, a number of statistical problems remain whenever FDI from the different countries is to be compared. The first issue concerns how FDI is registered. Two major alternatives are commonly found: one classifying the FDI according to the industry to which the investor belongs, the other classifying the FDI according to the industry to which the investment belongs. Hence, a real estate investment abroad by an engineering company may be labeled engineering investment or real estate investment, implying difficulties in our efforts to sort out the reaction of domestic manufacturing industries. Since classification by investing industry is the most frequently used principle and classification by investment industry is used only as additional information, we have had to report FDI by investing industry. Another distinction is between net and gross figures, where the net figures capture divestment in excess of the gross figures. We have used net figures for all countries.

The next problem concerns how to treat reinvested earnings. In the late 1980s, most of the countries conducted surveys to determine the size of reinvested earnings as a part of FDI. However, in general, the surveys cover only total FDI and provide no statements about how these earnings are distributed between sector and host country. Hence, in the comparisons provided by the figures, we have had to use FDI data excluding reinvested earnings.

We are also interested in company stocks of outward FDI. In some cases these stocks exist, while for other countries we have had to construct such figures based on cumulative net real FDI flows. Hence, the cumulative figures have to be interpreted with caution.

Finally, for some countries, not even proxies for outward FDI may be found when it comes to figures for sectors, host country and combinations of these. In these cases we have chosen to exhibit what we have found, although the data are found for just a few countries in our sample.

Appendix II

Exports per region 1987 and 1991

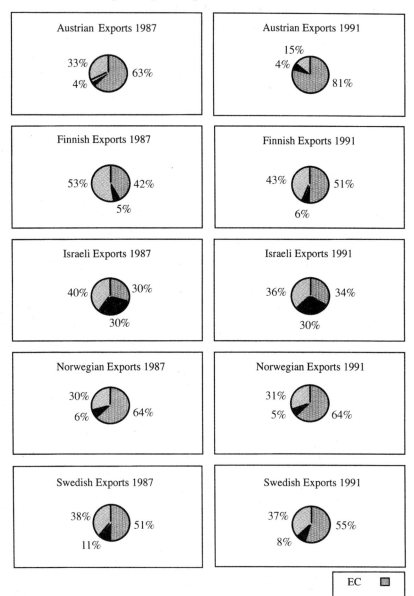

Austrian Exports 1987
33% 63% 4%

Austrian Exports 1991
15% 4% 81%

Finnish Exports 1987
53% 42% 5%

Finnish Exports 1991
43% 51% 6%

Israeli Exports 1987
40% 30% 30%

Israeli Exports 1991
36% 34% 30%

Norwegian Exports 1987
30% 6% 64%

Norwegian Exports 1991
31% 5% 64%

Swedish Exports 1987
38% 51% 11%

Swedish Exports 1991
37% 8% 55%

EC

US

Other

Source: Based on data from IMF.
Direction of Trade Statistics Yearbook 1993.

References

Baldwin, R.E., R. Forslid and J. Haaland. (1994): Investment Creation and Investment Diversion: Simulation Analysis of the Single Market Programme. *Mimeo*, Lund

Braunerhjelm, P. (1990) *Svenska Industriföretag Inför EG 1992*, Stockholm: Industrial Institute for Economic and Social Research.

Dunning, J. (1993): *Multinational Enterprises and the Global Economy*. Boston: Addison-Wesley.

IMF. (1993) *Direction of Trade Statistics Yearbook 1993*. Washington, DC: IMF.

Koivisto, J.V. (1993): *The Response of Finnish Industries to the Integration Process of EC: A Comparative Study between Schumpeter and Heckscher-Ohlin Industries*. Helsinki.

Markusen, J.R. (1994): Incorporating the Multinational Enterprise into the Theory of International Trade. *Mimeo*, NBER

Oxelheim, L. (1993): Foreign Direct Investment and the Liberalization of Capital Movements, in Oxelheim, L. (ed.) *The Global Race for Foreign Direct Investment*, Berlin: Springer-Verlag.

Ozawa, T. (1992): Cross-investment between Japan and the EC: Income Similarity, Product Variation and Economies of Scope, in Cantwell, J. (ed.) *Multinational Investment in Modern Europe: Strategic Interaction in the Integrated Community*, Brookfield: Edward Elgar Publishing Co.

Rugman, A. and S. Verbeke. (1991): Competitive Strategies for Non-European Firms, in Burgenmeier, B. and Mucchielli, J.L (eds.) *Multinationals and Europe 1992*, London: Routledge.

Sweeney, R. (1993): The International Competition for Foreign Direct Investment, in Oxelheim, L. (ed.) *The Global Race for Foreign Direct Investment in the 1990s*. Berlin: Springer Verlag.

UNCTAD. Division on Transnational Corporations and Investment. (1194): *World Investment Report 1994: Transnational Corporations, Employment and the Workplace*. New York: (United Nations publication Sales No. E.94.II.A.14).

US International Trade Commission. (1992): *The Effects of Greater Economic Integration within the European Community on the United States: Fourth Following Report*. Washington DC: US International Trade Commission.

Yamamaki, H. (1990): *Locational Decisions of Japanese Multinational Firms in European Manufacturing Industries*. *Mimeo*. Berlin: Science Center.

Yannopoulous, G. (1990): Foreign Direct Investment and European Integration: Evidence from the Formative Years of the European Community, *Journal of Common Market Studies* 28: 235-259.

Yannopoulous, G. (1992): Multinational Corporations and the Single European Market. In Cantwell, J. (ed.) *Multinational Investment in Modern Europe*. Brookfield: Edward Elgar Publishing Co.

Chapter 3:
Foreign Direct Investment from Small States and Integration

Micro- and Macroeconomic Evidence From Austria

Christian Bellak

The purpose of this chapter is to provide a case study of Austria's outsider response to the European single market program. Literature has emerged recently on the response of third country firms to the European Union (Acoccella 1990; Cantwell 1992; Eliasson and Lundberg 1989; Erbe, Grossman, Jungnickel, Koopmann and Scharrer 1991; Graham 1992; Greenaway 1993; Heitger and Stehn 1990; Hirsch and Almor 1992; Oxelheim and Braunerhjelm 1992; Rugman and Verbeke 1991; UNCTC 1990).Theoretical arguments have mainly concentrated on FDI as a preemptive move by firms towards political and economic integration. This process may be either defensive (Hirsch and Almor 1992) in order to hurdle barriers to entry (frontier controls, relative cost disadvantages, etc.), or of an offensive or strategic nature (Acoccella 1990). Both lead to a restructuring and concentration on elements of the value-added chain (economies of scale) as well as a relocation of activities.[16]

In an earlier investigation of Austria's response to the Union (Bellak 1992, c, d, 1994), most of the Hirsch and Almor hypotheses on outsider response were confirmed. With the single market, the deterioration of the relative competitive position of Austrian exporters leads to an increasing propensity to invest in the Union.

Outsider response to the Union involves a closely related issue, namely, the relationship between macro- and microintegration strategies. How are macro- and microintegration interrelated, and what effects can be

---

[16] Yannopoulos (1992: 331) mentions in addition that "the uncertainty generated by the harmonization at the Community level of 'grey-area' trade policy instruments increase(s) the attraction of producing inside the single market." Together with the danger of import-trade restrictions this will stimulate defensive, import-substituting FDI.

observed on the micro- and macroeconomic level? These two kinds of integration are discussed extensively by Dunning and Robson (1988). Macrointegration is defined as the (political and economic) integration of a state via an international treaty. Macrointegration may comprise various types of integration, ranging from a free-trade agreement (FTA), a customs union (CU), or a single market (SM), to an economic and monetary union (EMU). The (new) member of the integrating community is automatically put in an insider status. Microintegration (that is, exporting and foreign direct investment, FDI) is pursued by firms that are outsiders to the integrating community.

Since Austria has been member of EFTA from the 1960s, microintegration strategies were typical of its integration process in the European Union until the early 1990s. By its application for membership in 1987 and its membership in 1995, Austria approaches a new stage of integration; hence, the subject of this chapter – the role of microintegration via FDI (as an outsider) in the new stage of Austria's macrointegration (as an insider).

This chapter focuses on the following issues: a short survey of arguments presented in the literature on small states and both types of integration is presented in Section II. Section III assesses the question of economic benefits and costs of Austria's past and future macrointegration, as well as the strategies and economic benefits and costs of Austria's microintegration. Conclusions about the future competitiveness of Austrian firms and the relationship of micro- and macrointegration are presented in Section IV.

I. Integration of Small States

This chapter reviews the main hypotheses on macrointegration and microintegration in the case of a small open economy (SMOPEC). Since the classical work of Robinson (1960) on the Economic Consequences of the Size of Nations economists often have tried to distinguish small and large countries by economic characteristics (Andersson 1990; Walsh 1988; Bellak and Luostarinen 1994). The smallness of a country leads, *inter alia*, to various economic constraints, which affect trade, FDI and integration. This is not to say that smallness of a country is a source solely of disadvantages. Integration is, however, the main response in overcoming some of the constraints from smallness.

A. Constraints Caused by Smallness

Home Market

Small home-based demand leads to a lack of economies of scale-intensive industries. This may imply that there are only a few suppliers (in the case of non-exporters) and hence restrictions of competition, because minimum efficient technological scale is limited. "As a result, a small country is at a disadvantage in reaping the benefits of economies of scale and increasing returns" (Senjur 1992).[17] The small population of small countries leads to relative factor-cost disadvantages in labor-intensive industries (Breuss 1983) compared with well endowed countries.

The proximity of users to suppliers is a necessary (but not sufficient) pre-condition for the impulse to innovation in certain industries, or at least for the success of an innovation. Proximity is more easily achieved in small markets, but they do not provide enough incentives for innovation. *Ceteris paribus,* "there is a stronger incentive to commit resources to an innovation where the market is large than where it is small" (Walsh 1988).

Technological Capacity

The fact that the technological capacity of SMOPECs (Walsh 1987, 1988) is limited by resources and by markets that give few incentives to innovation, is enforced by the small country squeeze (Polt 1992; Walsh 1988: 49). The squeeze is based on two factors: (a) large countries with large R&D expenditures in new technologies and (b) newly industrialized countries (NICs) entering industries with low-cost production that were traditionally occupied by SMOPECs.[18]

Shortage of Resources

The lack of resources is also an obstacle to country-specific (market-specific) product differentiation and consequently to increasing economies of

[17] According to Schulmeister (1990), 52% of Austrian exports but 60% of imports can be regarded as economies-of-scale intensive in 1973 (1980: 53% and 58%; 1987: 67% and 63%). RCA values show a substantial gap in technology and human-capital intensive industries compared to other small countries (such as Switzerland). He concludes that despite a reduction of the gap during the 1970s, the share of resource-intensive products in exports decreased less than the OECD average during the 1980s. However, the result shows the nature of technology in SMOPECs and questions the role of the size of a country as a determinant of innovation and technology creation.

[18] Walsh (1988: 38f) presents arguments on the quick diffusion of new technologies in small countries (see also Polt 1992) which might be, according to her, an advantage of SMOPECs against large countries or "as an indication that it is not size so much as adaptability, flexibility and preparedness to develop appropriate production structures, which are the crucial factors." (Walsh 1988: 39).

scale. The resulting specialization strategy of SMOPECs is an advantage rather than a constraint, since market power and cost reductions may be achieved. Shortage of resources tends to reinforce the above mentioned lack of market-related innovation incentives.

A further conclusion may be drawn from the relatively smaller market power of SMOPEC firms: trade must be a second best option to integration for these firms. The reason being that competitors inside the market will be able to undercut the price charged by the outsider (Winckler 1989). This relatively lower price is caused by economies of scale as well as the absence of market barriers for insiders. Being an outsider, a SMOPEC does not gain from the economies of specialization as long as market barriers exist.

Trade Dependence

From the above arguments, it follows that SMOPECs would be price-takers in international markets rather than price-setters due to given terms of trade,[19] except in some niches. The export cost of SMOPECs should be higher than world export prices in general, because of relatively higher domestic production costs. The trade performance of SMOPECs should therefore be worse than in large countries (Hellmer 1988). Export prices are not dependent on the quantity exported, hence expansion of exports would not adversely affect terms of trade (Senjur 1992).

Combined, these push and pull factors (Luostarinen 1980) will have a greater influence on the decision to invest abroad in general because they are acting as constraints in SMOPECs (Bellak 1992), whereas in large countries they either do not exist at all (for example, small home market) or are of minor importance.

Economic Policy Range

The SMOPEC's macroeconomic policy range is extremely reduced (i) through the effects caused by structural change in other countries; (ii) by the dependence of the long term structural policy on a demand that is largely exogenous to the SMOPEC's economic policy (Borner 1986a) and (iii) since protectionist trade measures affect small and therefore trade-

---

[19] Except in highly specialized niches; for a discussion of the price-setter vs. price-taker issue in Austrian exports, see Marin (1983) and Dockner-Sitz (1986). Kramer (1991) notes that "the assumption of the exposed sector being a price-taker on international markets was an adequate description of this sector in the case of Austria until very recently". See also Steindl (1977).

dependent countries relatively stronger than large countries, application of such measures by small countries may lead to a substantial welfare loss in the case of a retaliatory policy by large countries. Moreover, growth of MNEs, as well as internationally interlinked and highly mobile capital markets (Rothschild 1989), lead to a loss of economic sovereignty of SMOPECs.

The main economic constraints arising from smallness have been summarized. In what follows, the idea is expounded that strategies to overcome these constraints are macrointegration, exporting and FDI. We shall discuss the effects of micro- and macrointegration strategies on the various constraints mentioned above.

B. SMOPECs and Integration

Concerning macrointegration, freetrade does not maximize the utility of a SMOPEC, because of the relatively higher risks involved in exporting compared with domestic sales. Further integration is needed to solve the problems of SMOPECs (Felderer 1974). Nevertheless, the effects of macrointegration could be asymmetrically distributed between large and small countries, because large firms from large countries benefit more than small countries with relatively smaller firms. As long as barriers exist, firms in small countries that cannot overcome the barriers will be relatively smaller. We find large firms also in small countries in industries with low trade or high entry barriers or with high FDI, licensing etc.

The aim for MNEs based in small, non-integrated countries is to overcome the many constraints (see above) via microintegration by extending the markets, the resources and the range of operations. MNEs from SMOPECs may, for example, overcome the resource shortage in R&D as well as the home market constraint by exporting. Thus, exporting is a necessary condition for R&D cost recoupment (Walsh 1988) and economies of scale (Breuss 1983).

Macrointegration itself exerts certain effects on microintegration. This influence has to be taken into account when interpreting exports and FDI of a small country. Trade-diversion and trade-creation effects as well as FDI-diversion and FDI-creation effects have to be considered. Table 8 summarizes the main effects. Although the net effect on trade is hard to predict on a theoretical level, the *ex ante* net effect on FDI, be it from insider or outsider firms seems to be positive. Clearly, the actual net effects may only be determined empirically. If it is true that SMOPECs, typically, are home countries to only a few MNEs as well as a large number of small firms, (or small scale industries: for example, Belderbos 1992; Ylä-Anttilla 1993; Breuss 1983) this will imply the following characteristics of SMOPECs and FDI:

- Walsh (1988) emphasizes economies of scale, long production runs and greater standardization as a requirement for exports by SMOPECs. The same reasoning might also apply in the case of investment abroad.
- At least the highly developed SMOPECs will have an additional incentive to internalize their comparative advantages, that is, to exploit knowledge-intensive and intangible assets via FDI, because these assets can hardly be separated from the firm (or entrepreneur), because of market failure.[20]
- Borner (1980, 1986a, 1986b) and others point out that smaller firms located in SMOPECs prefer an international (yet intrasectoral structural adaptation) to an intranational (yet intersectoral adaptation), because this leads to economies of multi-plant operation in the form of transferring market knowledge and experience stemming from exporting to FDI. According to him, this implies a relatively large share of cross-investments. The international, yet intrasectoral restructuring is also encouraged by the fact that new, complex technologies lead to niche strategies of small countries because of their resource shortage and the increasing subcontracting or assembly strategies of MNEs (see above). Rugman (1982) supports this argument with his conclusions that small Canadian firms will pursue subcontracting and specialized supplier strategies, so-called dependent strategies[21] (see also Walsh 1988).
- Firms from small countries will be relatively small if they are highly specialized, but not economies of scale-intensive producers. The market power of firms from small states will be lower if large-scale firms and industries prefer to be located in large countries. Suppliers from SMOPECs will therefore be at a disadvantage in intraindustry trade, because

---

[20] The argument rests on the fact that highly developed SMOPECs are highly specialized in some fields and their output shows a clear tendency to tertiarization (production-related services etc.). In this respect SMOPECs do, however, not differ from large countries.

[21] In the Austrian context an example is the automotive supplier industry. In certain years its export value was higher than the value of cars imported even though Austria does not have an automobile industry.

they cannot achieve the same scale, which translates into higher prices and ultimately into lower competitiveness.

• The relatively smaller production capacity creates a trade-off between diversification and market power (Breuss 1983). Therefore SMOPECs specialize in certain industries, concentrating their resources in a particular activity in order to gain market power. This leads to trade dependence and the risk of external shocks.

As a result of the above discussion, SMOPECs are generally assumed to concentrate on the following strategies: niches and specialization, inward investment by foreign MNEs, foreign investment, international cooperation, international structural adaptation. We shall see later on that these features are quite well reflected in Austria's strategy towards internationalization. These types of microintegration are thus a logical response of SMOPEC firms to various stages of macrointegration.

II. Austria's Integration

A. Stages of Integration via Trade

This subsection discusses effects of Austria's integration process, distinguishing between five stages: (1) Austria's EFTA membership, with some trade discrimination by the Community (1960-1972); (2) Austria's EFTA membership under the EFTA-Community free-trade agreement (1973-1977); (3) Austria's integration from 1978-1986; (4) Austria's EEA membership; and finally (5) Austria's Union membership. Thus we deal with *ex post* and *ex ante* integration effects. The focus of the *ex post* analysis is on trade effects of integration, since trade was the main field of Austrian integration up to the 1990s.

1960-1972
Already in the 1960s Austria's trade concentrated on Community countries. Hence the decision to join EFTA was seen as a political decision (Kramer 1991). During this period, trade-diversion effects arose, since the share of Austrian exports to the Community decreased by 11 percentage points and increased by 18 percentage points to EFTA between 1959 and 1972. Since EFTA markets are more distant, higher transport and transaction cost as well as sophisticated markets led to restructuring costs and

to "high efficiency and welfare losses" (Breuss 1992). The fact that Austria's trade balance with EFTA countries improved steadily implies a reduction of its negative, that is, low-tech, structural component. In this period Austria's share in the Community market decreased from 1.8% to 1.2%, while its EFTA market share increased from 0.6% to 1.9%.

1973-1976

The EFTA-Community free-trade agreement came into effect in 1973. Until 1977, Austria's trade was diverted towards the Community, and trade-creation effects arose. Trade-creation effects of EFTA were still important; Austria's market shares remained on a significantly higher level than before EFTA membership (Kramer 1991), resulting from a regional diversification of Austrian exports. The annual growthrate of Austrian exports to the present EFTA countries (in current prices) between 1960 and 1972 was 16.5%, and 6.2% from 1972 to 1989 (Kramer 1991). The share of Austrian exports to the Community increased by 7.3 percentage points, and the share of EFTA decreased by 9.7 percentage points (Dockner and Sitz quoted in Pichler 1992).[22] They estimate trade effects of integration on an industrial level and confirm the expected positive trade-creation effects with exports to the Community and the negative export and import effects with the EFTA. In some industries (textiles, machinery, electronics and vehicles) the negative EFTA effect outweighs the positive Community effect.

For the period 1960-1981, Breuss (1983) estimates the overall static integration effect as trade-diversion effects of 5.5% of GDP and trade-creation effects of 2.5% of GDP. Dynamic integration effects for this period were calculated (1) on the reduction of the productivity gap between Austria and Germany by four percentage points, resulting in an effect of 1% of GDP and (2) by the rising price level gap between Austria and Germany. Higher prices in Austria could lead to a reduction of consumer rents at about 5-7% of GDP (Breuss, Handler and Stankovsky 1988) compared with a scenario with equal prices as in Germany.

1978-1986

The further reduction of tariffs in the Tokyo Agreement of GATT led to a welfare loss of 0.3% of GDP, due to a reduction in Austria's high tariff levels that affected competition in exporting industries.

---

[22] For further details and methodology see Pichler, 1992: 249.

Table 8. Effects of macro integration on micro integration of outsiders.

Macroeconomic effect of integration	TNC strategic response of outsider **	Net trade effect	Net FDI effect
Intra-regional trade more attractive than extra regional trade *	Replace exports with foreign direct investment (defensive export substituting investment)	Sales by regionally-based TNC affiliates replace exports to the region by TNC (outsider) <	Increased investment in regionally based TNC affiliates >
New configuration of locational advantages among members of the region	Adjust existing investments in the region to reflect free intra-regional trade (Re-organization investment)	Intra regional trade could rise if reorganization leads to increased plant and country specialization. Extra regional exports could rise if regions' industries become more competitive in world markets. =>	for the region as a whole; gains in some countries offset by losses in others. =
Cost reduction and efficiency gains	Increase value-adding activities within region; integrate with other offshore investments (rationalized investment)	Same as for reorganization => but <= if less is imported into region	as TNCs increase sourcing in the region >
Market expansion, demand growth, and technical progress	Gain first-mover advantages via foreign direct investment (offensive export substituting investment)	If demand in regional market grows faster than supply from new inward FDI, = otherwise: <=	Same as for defensive export substituting investment >

>positive effect   < negative effect   = neutral   => neutral/possible positive effect   <= neutral/possible negative effect

* Assumes that integration does not result in lower external tariffs than previously existed among individual countries, and that non tariff barriers do not prevent the growth of intra regional trade.

** TNC ... Transnational Corporation(s)

Source: adapted from UNCTC, No. 15, 1990: 3

Another important aspect of tariff reduction and trade diversion towards the integrated region is the expected increase in intraindustry trade. ÖROK (1990, Nr. 84) has shown an increase of Austria's intraindustry-Community trade index from 53.6% to 70.0% between 1976 and 1986. Leading industries being the high-tech metal and the chemical sectors, while the textile and the low-tech metal sector are the most specialized industries. The share of Community in Austrian exports increased by 19 percentage points between 1973 and 1991 (Breuss 1992). The free trade agreement led to similar import-export growth effects of integration, as in the pre-EFTA membership stage.

The main integration effects in the past were thus trade related. Since trade has been fully liberalized, future integration effects will have other sources.

Concerning *ex ante* effects of integration, the Austrian Institute of Economic Research (WIFO) has calculated medium-term macro- and microeconomic effects with the Cecchini Report model (Breuss, Handler and Stankovsky 1988; Breuss and Stankovsky 1988; Breuss and Schebeck 1989, 1991; Breuss 1992, Breuss and Kitzmantel 1993). Three scenarios were created: Austria remaining an EFTA member, Austria joining the EEA, and Austria becoming a member of the Union. The results of the calculations are shown in Table 9. It is far beyond the scope of this chapter to discuss the various effects or their plausibility in detail (Breuss and Schebeck 1991, a, b). Since we are primarily interested in the outsider response to EC 92 and its relation to microintegration of firms, we will only discuss effects of Union membership in greater detail.

B. EFTA membership and EEA membership

Theoretically, even if Austria had stayed outside the EEA, Austria would gain from the trade-creation effects of the single market. Integration via trade, as well as via FDI in the Union, stimulates growth, yet FDI dampens growth to the extent that trade and domestic investment substitute each other.

Not surprisingly, the growth effects of EEA integration are somewhat higher (Table 9) than in the EFTA membership scenario, yet lower than in the Union membership scenario, due to discrimination in some fields.

Table 9. Macroeconomic effects: EFTA, EEA and European Union compared from basic model.

Year	EFTA						EEA						EU					
	(1)	(2)	(3)	(4)	(5)	(6)	(1)	(2)	(3)	(4)	(5)	(6)	(1)	(2)	(3)	(4)	(5)	(6)
Consumption: private	0.2	0.5	0.8	1.0	1.3	1.5	0.1	0.4	0.8	1.1	1.4	1.7	0.5	1.3	3.0	2.6	3.1	3.5
Consumption: public	0.1	0.3	0.5	0.7	0.8	0.9	0.3	0.7	1.1	1.3	1.5	1.6	0.7	1.5	1.9	2.2	2.3	2.4
Gross capital formation	-0.2	0.4	1.0	1.4	1.7	2.0	-0.2	1.1	2.4	3.4	4.2	5.0	0.2	2.4	4.3	5.7	6.6	7.4
Exports	1.6	3.1	4.0	4.4	5.1	5.7	1.8	3.4	4.3	4.7	5.5	6.1	3.1	5.3	6.6	7.2	8.1	8.7
Goods	2.2	4.0	4.9	5.1	6.0	6.6	2.5	4.4	5.3	5.6	6.5	7.1	3.9	6.3	7.7	8.2	9.3	10.1
Tourism	-0.1	1.0	2.0	2.9	3.4	3.8	0.0	1.1	2.2	3.0	3.4	3.8	1.4	3.5	4.8	5.6	6.0	6.3
Imports	1.0	2.5	3.5	4.2	4.8	5.3	1.0	2.6	3.8	4.6	5.4	6.0	2.6	5.1	6.8	8.0	9.0	9.7
Goods	1.2	2.7	3.7	4.2	4.9	5.3	1.1	2.9	4.1	4.8	5.6	6.2	3.1	5.9	7.7	8.8	9.8	10.4
Tourism	0.7	2.5	4.6	6.2	7.2	8.1	0.6	1.7	3.8	5.4	6.5	7.3	0.4	1.7	4.5	6.4	8.0	9.2
GDP real	0.3	0.7	1.0	1.2	1.4	1.5	0.4	1.0	1.4	1.7	2.1	2.3	0.7	1.8	2.4	2.9	3.3	3.6
Current account as % of GDP	0.3	0.5	0.6	0.7	0.7	0.7	0.2	0.3	0.4	0.3	0.3	0.3	-0.7	-0.9	-1.2	-1.4	-1.4	-1.4
Consumer prices	-0.3	-0.7	-1.1	-1.5	-1.7	-1.8	-0.7	-1.5	-2.3	-2.8	-3.1	-3.4	-1.8	-3.4	-4.3	-4.8	-5.0	-5.2
Terms of trade: goods	0.4	0.8	1.3	1.5	1.7	1.8	0.2	0.5	0.9	1.2	1.3	1.4	-0.4	-0.7	-0.9	-1.0	-1.0	-1.1
Net income	0.1	0.2	0.1	0.0	0.0	0.0	-0.6	-0.7	-1.0	-1.1	-1.2	-1.2	-0.7	-1.0	-1.3	-1.2	-1.1	-1.1
Wage rate	-0.1	-0.1	-0.1	-0.1	-0.1	-0.1	0.0	0.0	0.1	0.2	0.2	0.3	0.1	0.0	0.1	0.2	0.4	0.6
Employment: in 1000 employes	2.7	6.8	10.6	13.8	17.3	20.6	-7.2	1.5	9.6	16.6	23.6	29.8	-5.4	5.1	17.1	28.6	39.1	47.5
in %	0.1	0.2	0.4	0.5	0.6	0.7	-0.3	0.1	0.3	0.6	0.8	1.1	-0.2	0.2	0.6	1.0	1.4	1.7
Unemployment rate	-0.1	-0.2	-0.2	-0.3	-0.4	-0.4	0.3	0.0	-0.2	-0.3	-0.5	-0.6	0.3	0.0	-0.3	-0.6	-0.8	-1.0
Labour-productivity of private sector	0.2	0.5	0.6	0.6	0.7	0.7	0.8	1.0	1.1	1.1	1.1	1.1	1.0	1.6	1.7	1.7	1.6	1.5
State deficit as % of GDP	0.0	0.1	0.1	0.1	0.2	0.2	0.1	0.2	0.2	0.3	0.4	0.5	-1.2	-1.3	-1.3	-1.2	-1.1	-1.0

Source: Breuss and Schebeck (1991)

The figures are percentage differences from basic model. For example, the basic model predicts a GDP growth of 2 % for a certain year. One must add the figure in the table to get to total GDP growth in the various scenarios.

C. Union membership

The full integration of Austria into the Union on 1 January 1995 should lead to GDP growth (3.5% medium-term), employment etc. (Table 9). However, Austria will have to pay "the 'price' for a good performance on the goods and labor markets (with) rather high deficits in the external and internal balance" (Breuss, Handler and Stankowsky 1989). Most authors emphasize that future integration effects will be based on dynamic (that is, productivity growth and intensified competition) rather than on static (that is, trade; Baldwin 1992) effects, since Austria's microintegration via exports has already reached a high level.

In order to gain from dynamic effects, the Austrian economy will have to bear the cost of substantial restructuring in certain sectors. Bayer (1991, 1992) examined the so-called sensitive sectors (for the concept, see Buigues and Ilzkovitz 1989) of the Austrian economy, defined as sectors protected by nontariff trade barriers. They account for 45% of employees and 41% of value added of the manufacturing sector. With regard to competitiveness, one third of employees are working in sensitive sectors, two-fifth in sectors with balanced competitiveness *vis-à-vis* foreign competitors and nearly 25% in comparatively weak sectors, that is, subsectors of the chemical, electronics, food, textiles and clothing industries (Bayer 1991).

Another important fact is the relevance of the sheltered sector of the Austrian economy (for example, state monopolies, insurance, banking, telecommunications, transport). First, it is important because of its size, which is shown by the OECD (1990) estimates that up to 50% of total value added originated in some sort of sheltered sector; and second, because the main adaptation cost will fall on the sheltered sector.

In order to understand the role of the sheltered sector one has to know about its particular relationship to the open sector. If the open sector is charged higher than competitive prices by the service-supplying sheltered sector, not only terms of trade are affected adversely, but also producer and consumer rent is redistributed to the sheltered sector. This and other structural disadvantages support economic arguments for integration – yet restructuring would have to continue also in the EFTA membership scenario. The full opening of the sheltered sector (public procurement etc.) will tend to reduce the gap of prices and costs between Austria and the Union via enhanced competition. Taking as an indicator the resulting increase in consumer rent as a percentage of GDP, Breuss, Handler and Stankovsky (1988) estimate a potential of 5.5%. In other research, Guger, Handler and Stankovsky (1990) and Wieser (1989) give examples of price differences compared with other countries, due to restricted competition in Austria.

It is argued that enhanced competition and economies of scale will lead to a narrowing of the productivity gap between Austria and the Union. In 1992 Austria's productivity, however, equaled that of the Union average after a strong catch-up process during the 1980s. Breuss, Handler and Stankovsky (1988) estimated a potential welfare gain of 10% of GDP, assuming an 18% gap between Austria and Germany due to the productivity increase. The productivity gap between its main trading partner, Germany was reduced substantially during the 1980s. The gap, which was about 32% in 1970, has been successively reduced to 1% in 1991 (Guger 1992). Adding micro- (5% of GDP) and macroeconomic (3.5% of GDP) effects, they show a similar relationship to those of the Cecchini Report.[23]

D. Stages of Integration via FDI [24]

We have defined microintegration strategies as exporting and FDI. As the single market comes into effect, outsiders are put at a disadvantage with exporting as an integration strategy. Therefore we concentrate on Austrian FDI in the Union, distinguishing between three main periods. The second part of the subsection discusses the main effects of outward FDI on Austria.[25]

Pre 1987

The period from the 1960s up to 1987 was marked by larger inward than outward FDI flows. Annual outward flows were on a relatively low level, not exceeding ATS 3.3 billion (with the exception of 1986; Figure 20). As a result, inward stocks were considerably larger than outward stocks, either measured as accumulated flows from balance of payments (Figure 19) or as book values (Table 10).

Up to 1987, accumulated outward stocks were ATS 30 billion, inward ATS 58 billion; book-values outward were ATS 15 billion, inward ATS 74 billion. It follows that accumulated stocks are larger than book values with

---

[23] Breuss, Handler and Stankovsky (1988: 43 FN 4) emphasize that the microeconomic effects (lowering the productivity gap and the price-level gap vis-à-vis Germany) would bear a potential welfare-gain of 10% of GDP.

[24] This section is based on Bellak (1992a).

[25] Austrian FDI data are either obtained from balance of payments statistics or from Central Bank surveys conducted biannually.

outward FDI, but smaller with inward FDI.[26] Since the response ratio does not differ with inward and outward FDI, book values are more close to the real picture, not just because of valuation adjustments. Taking the period 1980-1990, inward and outward flows were balanced, inward stocks showing only half the average annual growth-rate of outward stocks, albeit starting from a higher level.

The comparatively low level of Austrian FDI abroad has been explained *inter alia* by the following factors: Bellak, Fischer, Podesser and Schönhofer, 1989; Bellak and Oettl 1990; Proske 1989; Urban 1989; Bellak, 1992a; Pichl, 1989a, b; IWI 1990.

- Austrian firms were able to increase their market share in the Union via exporting. Tariff jumping via FDI was not necessary. Because of the structure of exports, mainly semimanufactured and investment goods, tariff barriers played a minor role.
- The large inward investment reduces the potential for outward investment in some industries (for example, electronics, which is dominated by foreign subsidiaries such as Siemens, ABB, Philips, IBM etc.).
- There is a lack of ownership advantages (Bellak and Weiss 1992, 1993), of which the structural trade-balance deficit mentioned above may be an indicator.
- A substantial share of the public company Austrian Industries AG in the manufacturing industry, which created an ideological barrier to FDI as a job-exporting mechanism.
- A chronically low equity-capital ratio, increasing only slightly between 1980 (19.2%) and 1990 (22.6%).
- The lack of a long-term strategic industrial policy as well as interfirm rivalry prevented so-called Austrian solutions, that is, the creation of large conglomerates that could bear the risk of large-scale internationalization (for example, pulp and paper; ski equipment).
- A slow restructuring process at home etc.

Factors encouraging FDI were market-seeking motives as well as insecurity about the future integration strategy of the government.

---

[26] To a certain extent this may be explained by local funding of inward FDI as well as reinvested profits, yet this can only be part of the substantial balance.

Figure 19. Austrian FDI stocks (accumulated from balance of payments) in millions of ATS.

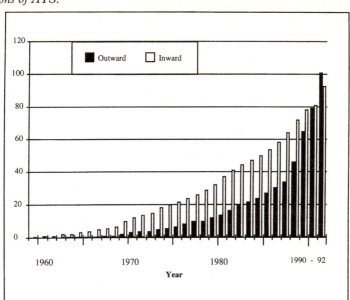

Note: For definition of FDI flows, see note on Figure 20.

The low level of outward FDI may be shown with the level-of-development approach (Dunning 1981). This approach relates per capita GDP to net outward investment (NOI)[27] and forecasts a positive NOI for highly developed countries (Figure 21). The figure shows unequivocally that, despite an increase in Austria's per capita income, a stronger outward FDI orientation did not evolve for a long time.

A few indicators should give a rough picture of the main features of Austrian FDI (Bellak 1992a) and serve as a basis for the description of the subsequent periods. The main sectors engaging in FDI were: the food and construction industry, in relative terms[28]; and the metal and the chemical sector, in absolute terms (1990). Against the international trend, the man-

---

[27] Calculated by gross inward (GII) minus gross outward (GOI) investment.
[28] Measured by FDI per employee. Note that the sectoral distribution must be interpreted with caution, because it does not follow the three-sector classification. Only two sectors, manufacturing and non-manufacturing, are distinguished, containing overlaps and unclassified activities. As a result, industry and sector data are comparable neither to statistics on the domestic manufacturing sector nor to SITC data.

Figure 20. Austrian FDI flows (balance of payments) in millions of ATS.

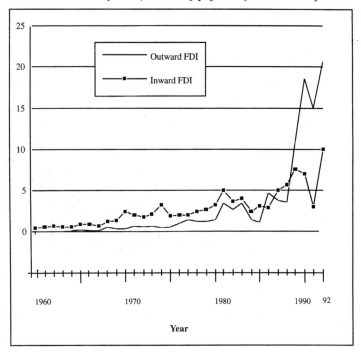

Note: FDI flows are net flows from balance of payments excluding reinvested earnings

ufacturing sector extended its share relative to the non-manufacturing (that is, mainly the service) sector between 1980 (43.3%) and 1987 (66.2%), which might be explained by divestment of the service sector, partly as a change in the long-term debt position and partly due to the lack of competition in many service subsectors. The shares of certain industries vary substantially because of single transactions, taking the small amount of capital involved into account.

FDI was regionally concentrated, mainly following the export flows. The Union accounted for 52% and EFTA for 21% of total nominal capital stock abroad. Germany (32.5%), the United States (16.7%) and Switzerland (20.7%) received 70% of the total stock in 1986. These countries are also the main inward investors. For example, German companies had 1,373 subsidiaries with a turnover of ATS 213 billion and 119,000 employees in Austria by 1986 (Goldmann 1991). Austria depends on Germany not only in exports, but also in FDI. It was not until 1986 that the

Figure 21. "Level of Development" 1972-1992.

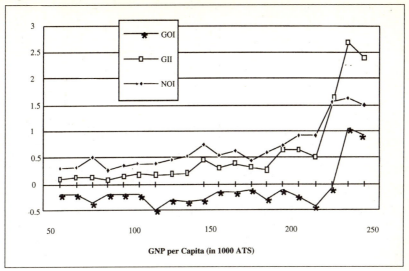

GOI: gross outward investment flow
GII: gross inward investment flow
NOI: net outward investment flow = GOI - GII.
See text for details

net FDI ratio[29] became positive. In 1970 it was -0.72, in 1980 -0.18 and in 1986 +0.04. In this respect Austria is, according to Walsh, a typical SMOPEC relying mainly on inward investment.

Outward FDI as a percentage of exports reached 1% only recently (1980: 0.53%; 1985: 0.28%; 1986: 1.32%), confirming exports as a dominant strategy of microintegration. Outward FDI flows compared with domestic investment amounted to 0.5% in 1980 and 0.4% in 1985 (1985 prices). Even if part of the outward FDI substituted for domestic investment or exports, its effects on output and employment were negligible. Outward FDI stocks as a percentage of GDP were well below the international average, barely reaching 2% in 1987 (1985: 1.4%). To provide a comparison to trade, exports reached 26% of GDP and imports 32% of GDP in 1986. FDI in eastern Europe is not included in these data, since they are mostly joint ventures, sometimes with minority holdings, sometimes without equity participation and thus not defined as FDI by the Central Bank. The strategic value of FDI in eastern Europe is therefore not adequately represented by the data at hand.

[29] Calculated as outward minus inward FDI as percentage of GDP.

Table 10.   Outward FDI stocks (book values) in millions of ATS.

Year	Manufacturing		Non-manufacturing		Total	
	Number	Capital	Number	Capital	Number	Capital
1980	159	3,167	166	4,253	325	7,320
1981	367	4,575	318	5,504	685	10,079
1982	370	5,346	354	5,933	724	11,279
1983	432	7,083	390	6,582	822	13,665
1984	463	8,513	435	7,943	898	16,455
1985	291	10,647	450	7,999	941	18,646
1986	513	8,598	502	8,116	1,015	16,714
1987	525	9,936	503	5,079	1,028	15,015
1988	590	11,483	580	5,602	1,170	17,085
1989	491	16,606	348	13,747	839	30,353
1990	665	28,069	462	17,559	1,127	45,628
1991	717	40,102	4706	19,636	1,187	59,737

Note: In 1989 the number of FDI decreased due to a reduction of surveyed firms, yet the stock increased.

Apart from monetary indicators, one should use real indicators to assess the relevance of inward and outward FDI. The number of Austrian subsidiaries abroad was 1,015 (513 in the manufacturing sector) in 1986, while the number of foreign subsidiaries in Austria was 2,267 (747 in the manufacturing sector). Figures on employment in Austrian subsidiaries abroad are available only from 1980 (see Table 11). The relationship of employment in inward and outward FDI (4.3:1) resembles the relationship of FDI stocks (1988: 5:1). The share of foreign to domestic employment is about 2% for outward and about 9% for inward FDI during the 1980s (manufacturing sector: 6% and 27% respectively). The manufacturing sector employed 35,000 people abroad, while 149,000 employees can be attributed to foreign-controlled subsidiaries in Austria in 1986.

These characteristics taken together lead to the conclusion that internationalization during the pre-1987 period had little importance for outward FDI, yet substantial importance for inward FDI. On the outward side, investors were mainly concentrated in three industries (metals, chemicals, and banking/finance/insurance), accounting for 75% of FDI stock, while inward investment was more evenly distributed among industries. Regarding overall FDI, this led to an unbalanced development, since inward FDI grew rapidly during the 1970s and 1980s, taking advantage of infrastructure, subsidies, political and social stability, labor cost etc. (Glatz and Moser 1989a).

Table 11. Employment in Austrian FDI.

	Total	Outward FDI Weighted by Austrian share in foreign capital					Inward FDI (direct)
		total	-25%	26-50%	51-80%	80%-	total
1985							
Manufacturing	30,845	12,197	1,431	3,340	693	6,733	157,000
Non-manufacturing	29,197	9,965	1,260	727	1,601	6,377	84,000
total	60,042	22,162	2,691	4,067	2,294	13,100	241,000
1986							
Manufacturing	34,673	12,905	1,610	3,556	678	7,061	149,000
Non-manufacturing	30,351	10,653	1,342	769	1,796	6,746	109,000
total	65,024	23,558	2,952	4,325	2,474	13,807	258,000
1987							
Manufacturing	35,255	14,051	1,352	3,518	988	8,193	149,000
Non-manufacturing	22,777	9,359	353	1,056	1,557	6,393	99,000
total	58,032	23,410	1,705	4,574	2,545	14,586	248,000
1988							
Manufacturing	37,186	15,111	1,295	4,099	1,239	8,478	146,000
Non-manufacturing	23,685	10,304	382	1,219	1,727	6,976	116,000
total	60,871	25,415	1,677	5,318	2,966	15,454	262,000
1989							
Manufacturing	40,484	21,311	1,245	4,333	4,249	11,484	159,000
Non-manufacturing	13,863	10,297	225	1,816	1,546	6,710	124,000
total	54,347	31,608	1,470	6,149	5,759	18,194	283,000
1990							
Manufacturing	57,745	30,766	1,976	7,149	6,101	15,540	167,000
Non-manufacturing	24,546	17,064	680	3,020	4,150	9,214	124,000
total	82,291	47,830	2,656	10,169	10,251	24,754	291,000
1991							
Manufacturing	59,509	41,182	991	9,559	10,467	20,165	145,000
Non-manufacturing	40,733	32,111	828	3,144	13,520	14,619	117,000
total	100,242	73,293	1,819	12,703	23,987	34,784	262,000

Source: Central Bank Surveys

The weighted employment figures reflect the number of employees attributable to the Austrian share in the foreign subsidiary, while the total (in column 1) shows all employment in foreign subsidiaries and thus is larger than the sum of weighted employment, since many subsidiaries abroad are not 100% owned.

1987-1992

The direction of FDI flows changed dramatically in 1987. Outward flows exploded and inward flows stagnated. The outward stock grew at an average annual rate of 25.3%; the inward stock grew only 8.7% annually (Figure 20). This development resulted in a balancing of accumulated stocks in 1992, which shows the strong catch-up process. Yet, in 1987 the amount of outward stock was only 52% of inward stock. Two factors lead to this process:

- The Union single market was definitely planned to come into effect in 1992. This would put Austrian firms in a relatively disadvantageous position through entry barriers to Union markets (see Hirsch and Almor 1992). By far the largest part of the additional FDI in this period was transferred to the Union to acquire or set up firms there.
- The opening of the traditional export markets in eastern Europe for FDI: naturally, the central location of Austria, as well as the structural trade balance deficit with Western countries, favored trade with eastern Europe in the past. Market growth as well as a learning-curve effect led to increased trade and Austrian FDI in these regions. Concerning eastern European FDI, a caveat should be made: figures on nominal capital shown in Table 10 do not include joint-ventures in eastern Europe. Statistics of home and host countries differ substantially. The number of Austrian joint ventures has increased dramatically (1991: 3,500; 1990: 955; 1989: 330), yet the capital transfer involved was very low. Seventy percent of the subsidiaries were sales units; less than 30% were production units. The main host country was still Hungary, with an estimated stock of ATS 8 billion in 1991 (Stankovsky 1992). Again, large firms were engaged in joint ventures: firms with a turnover of more than ATS 1 billion accounted for 60% of FDI, small firms for only 12%.

Yet, there is a third reason for the dramatic upswing of outward FDI, which was caused by a few major acquisitions of Austrian manufacturing firms abroad. The 20 largest manufacturing firms (see Table 12), of which nine would fulfill the Harvard criteria on MNEs (Siegel 1992), accounted for 75% of total employment abroad in 1989, according to the Central Bank (manufacturing sector) (Bellak 1992c). There was no explicit industry concentration discernible. With 669 FDIs abroad, altogether these firms had almost all of the total subsidiaries of the manufacturing sector reported by the Central Bank in 1990 (665).

Table 12. The 30 largest Austrian multinational groups in 1991 (manufacturing sector).

		Turnover millions of ATS	Employees	Employees abroad (e)	Industry
1	Austrian Industries AG	169,776	78,689	11,841	Metals, petroleum refining, industrial equipment
2	Steyr-Daimler-Puch AG	18,961	8,878	-	Motor vehicles
3	Constantia Industrieholding AG	11,400	6,218	2,600	Chemicals, misc.
4	Swarovski-Gruppe	11,017	9,328	3,247	Jewelry, watches, misc.
5	Wienerberger Baustoffind. AG	10,528	5,137	960	Building materials
6	Frantschach AG (a)	10,489	5,494	2,554	Pulp & paper
7	Österreichische Brau-Beteiligungs AG	9,200	6,232	-	Beverages
8	Radex-Heraklith Ind. Bet .AG	9,012	5,919	1,126	Building material
9	Mayr-Melnhof-Gruppe	8,012	3,350	-	Pulp & paper
10	Lenzing-Gruppe	7,508	5,775	857	Chemicals
11	Prinzhorn-Gruppe (b)	ca. 7,500	ca. 6,500	-	Pulp & paper, chemicals
12	M. Kaindl Holzindustrie (c,d)	7,000	1,800	1,300	Forest products
13	Agrana Beteiligungs-AG (a)	5,718	1,752	-	Food
14	Fritz Egger GmbH	5,700	1,800	1,067	Forest products
15	Perlmooser-Gruppe	5,351	3,863	-	Building material
16	Austria Tabakwerke AG (c)	5,015	2,029	-	Tobacco
17	Umdasch Industrie AG (a)	4,097	3,390	1,030	Building material
18	Engel Firmengruppe (a)	3,730	2,253	500	Industrial equipment
19	Zumtobel Holding AG	3,671	2,911	551	Electronics
20	Greiner Holding AG	3,520	2,401	873	Chemicals
21	Plansee Metall AG (a)	3,350	2,858	763	Metal products
22	Auricon Beteiligungs-AG	3,343	2,525	-	Industrial equipment
23	Nettingsdorfer Papierf. AG	3,181	1,414	462	Pulp & paper
24	Kapsch AG	3,150	2,238	-	Electronics
25	Montana AG	3,100	1,100	-	Chemicals
26	Plasser & Theurer GmbH (d)	3,000	1,280	1,700	Industrial equipment
27	Blum Verwaltungs GmbH (a)	2,997	1,898	219	Metal products
28	Vogel & Noot AG	2,935	1,577	-	Industrial equipment
29	Steyrermühl Papier AG	2,897	725	-	Pulp and paper
30	Waagner Biró AG	2,434	1,984	-	Industrial equipment
	Total	347,592	181,318	-	-

(a) 1991/1992; (b) not consolidated; (c) 1990; (d) Austrian firms only; (e) 1990; (-) ....
not available.
Source: adapted from Siegel (1993)

These large firms are dominated by a single public company, Austrian Industries AG, which accounted for 48.8% of the turnover and 43.4% of the employees of the 30 largest firms in 1991 (based on Siegel 1993). Austrian Industries AG invested ATS 6.4 billion in 1989 and ATS 7.4 billion in 1990, and hence about 40% of total investment abroad (even higher if only the manufacturing sector was taken as a basis for calculation). As

Bach (1992) noted, the company invested heavily abroad again in 1992. The company employed 12,000 people abroad (1990; 1991: 16,000) and accounted for 40% of production units (106) and 55% of sales subsidiaries (219) of the 20 largest manufacturing Austrian MNEs. The public company had production units in more than 23 countries and sales subsidiaries in more than 40 countries.

The development may also be shown by using the same indicators as for the pre-1987 period. FDI as a percentage of exports reached 4.4% in 1992, which shows the strong catch-up process of FDI, some of which is export-substituting (see below) at an increasing proportion and value. Outward flows exceeded inward flows in 1989 by 3.6, 1990 by 11.2, 1991 by 11.9 and 1992 by ATS 11.8 billion. Compared with domestic investment, FDI flows reached 4.3% in 1992, which is about four times the value of 1987 flows (1.1%). Substitution of domestic investment by FDI seemed to have increased (see Effects below) and is no longer negligible.

Outward FDI stocks as a percentage of the GDP more than doubled between 1987 and 1992, reaching 5% in 1992 (1991: 4.1%; 1989: 2.8%). Assuming a constant capital-output ratio, this implied a growth of foreign and a partial reduction of domestic activities. Employment in the FDI of the manufacturing sector abroad doubled between 1985 and 1990 (latest available figure: 57,745; total: 82,291 employees). This was mainly a result of acquisition strategies rather than greenfield investment (see below).

Employment in inward FDI rose to 291,000 (167,000 in the manufacturing sector). Yet although inward investment stagnated during the period 1987-1992, on average it increased – especially in 1992 and 1993. The accumulated stock of inward investment from three decades reached its highest level since the 1960s, despite some major divestment. Forty percent of foreign nominal capital was held by German investors in 1989 (up 146% since 1979), 16% by holding companies in Switzerland/Liechtenstein and 11% by the Netherlands. In absolute terms, foreign nominal capital more than doubled during these 10 years (Beer, Ederer, Goldmann, Lang, Passweg and Reitzner 1989). Sixty-two percent of foreign capital originated from the Union and 19.9% from the EFTA; 43% of foreign capital was invested in the manufacturing sector in 1989. The share of nominal capital owned by foreign investors varied considerably between sectors: 51% in the insurance industry, 30% in the manufacturing and service sector, but only 14% of the banking sector.

The number of outward acquisitions by Austrian firms between 1986 and 1990 was 40 (Arbeiterkammer 1989), showing a tendency to increase;

72% of acquisitions were made in the Union and 13% in EFTA. Germany (36% of acquisitions) and the United States as well as Hungary and the Czech Republic, were the leading countries (Bayer and Wetzel 1992).

As a consequence, intraindustry direct investment (IIDI, Table 13) increased in all manufacturing industries (1990 compared with 1980). A modest increase of the index occurred in the metal/vehicles sector, where inward and outward investment increased. Examples of increase in the index due to rising inward investment without substantial outward investment were the electronics, the food and the textile industries. A substantial increase in inward and outward FDI was revealed for the petrochemicals and the wood/paper industries.

Prior to 1987, market-seeking investment dominated. With the application for Austrian membership in the Union and the single market approaching, the external environment even for exposed sector firms changed and with it the motives for FDI. Expecting EEA or even Union membership, firms started to rationalize their Europe-wide activities, efficiency seeking motives dominated as well as strategic asset seeking FDI. In particular, vertical and horizontal mergers helped to increase the scale (and in some cases the scope) of activities and enabled firms to concentrate certain activities in specific locations. The increasingly used international division of labor allowed firms to increase their specialization and create barriers to entry. Other motives for membership in the Union were to support exports, to be present in future markets in eastern Europe, and – of minor importance – cost-reducing relocation to eastern European countries (depending on the productivity of the respective firm or industry). For example, the company Wienerberger AG bought seven firms in Germany, leading to a monopolistic position there in construction material. Austrian Airlines, which had a quasi-monopoly position until recently, has been searching for cooperation around the globe.[30] Mayr-Melnhof has become one of the world's leading cardboard manufacturers by acquiring several producers throughout Europe.

Austria's FDI structure is thus in line with the above argument that small countries tend to have few true MNEs and that they pursue a strategy of inward investment. Since the share of cross investments[31] of the

---

[30] In the newspapers it was reported that there is still some nationalistic sentiment about selling (parts of) 'our' companies.
[31] A cross investment is a subsidiary in an industry other than the parent company: for example, a producer of chemicals sets up a research or sales subsidiary abroad.

Table 13. *Intra-industry direct investment in Austria 1980 and 1990 (millions of ATS).*

Industry	Outward stock		Inward stock		(O+I)		|O-I|		[(O+I)-|O-I|]/(O+I)	
	1980	1990	1980	1990	1980	1990	1980	1990	1980	1990
Metal, vehicles	1,880	5,942	4,841	12,162	6,721	18,104	2,961	6,220	0.559	0.656
Electronics	64	901	5,541	6,254	5,605	7,155	5,477	5,353	0.023	0.252
(Petro) Chemicals	571	7,746	7,117	14,022	7,688	21,768	6,546	6,276	0.149	0.712
Wood, paper	185	1,597	1,046	2,526	1,231	4,123	861	929	0.301	0.775
Textiles, clothing	127	403	1,605	2,792	1,732	3,195	1,478	2,389	0.147	0.252
Food	325	2,109	2,539	1,532	2,864	3,641	2,214	577	0.164	0.842
Ceramics, construction	15	1,651	1,368	4,040	1,383	5,691	1,353	2,389	0.022	0.580

Index = 1 ... all direct investment may be termed as 'intraindustry'. Both inward and outward investment are either high or low.
An increase of the indicator between 1980 and 1990 shows a reduction of the imbalance between inward and outward direct investments.
Index = 0 ... no intraindustry direct investment

See "Austrias integration" for the respective intraindustry trade index.

manufacturing sector is rather high in distribution, as we have shown elsewhere (Bellak 1992a), we support Borner's view of international intrasectoral restructuring of (small) SMOPEC firms. A large share in trade via
foreign subsidiaries points to a lack of country-specific differentiation,
since the same product is sold in more markets, rather than a differentiat-
ed product in one market. Since growth via FDI is one of the main strategies of some Austrian firms, they will have lower adaptation cost to bear
in the case of further macrointegration – they are already insiders. The
probability of using the market potential effectively is much higher with
the former than the latter, because knowledge of markets and competitors
is already given. Macrointegration supports the microintegration effects
and vice versa.

Post-1992

There are several instances that let us expect a continuation of the post-
1987 trend, albeit there have been some countervailing forces in inward as
well as outward investment at work. Regarding inward investment first,
the above reported boom of foreign acquisitions will increase average
annual flows, yet foreign firms were still reluctant to make greenfield
investments as Austria was still an outsider. Bayer and Wetzel (1992) concluded that even if Austria stayed outside the Union, inward FDI would
be advantageous, because it could still serve the Austrian and eastern
European markets. In a survey (Pichl 1989c), 20% of respondents tended
to believe that they would be bought by a foreign company, even the more
so, if Austria joined the Union.

Concerning outward investment expectations, market growth in anticipation of Union membership as well as the fear of remaining outside the
Union and the lack of economies of scale tends to increase annual FDI
flows. On the other hand, the ongoing sell-out of Austrian firms to foreign
firms reduces the potential of outward investments (since subsidiaries usually invest less abroad than holding companies), and some firms will enter
into a consolidation phase (Bellak 1992a) after restructuring their activities. In general, it is thus safe to assume that microintegration is growing
at a faster rate in the 1990s, especially in FDI but also in exports.

III. Effects of Outward and Inward FDI on the Austrian Economy [32]

In the past, we have observed a (changing) political perception of MNEs and their effects entering a new phase in the 1990s. The 1960s job-export debate (MNEs as agents of imperialism) was followed by a more positive attitude in the 1970s and 1980s (MNEs conquering markets), and again a more critical stance towards MNEs in the 1990s (MNEs as agents of integration and exporters of competitive advantages). Since we have already assessed the effects of integration on trade we concentrate on effects of FDI on the home country in the following subsections. Only a few empirical studies[33] are available internationally, and theoretical models[34] are mostly partial.

The Political Economy of Partial Effects

Apart from mere economic effects, there are certain important political effects of FDI – mainly the sovereignty loss of a SMOPEC that is dominated by large MNEs.[35] With the steadily rising inward FDI stock in Austria (see above), the controversy about the best relation between foreign

---

[32] For a detailed discussion of effects of outward FDI on the home country see Bellak, 1993.

[33] For example: the United States: Adler and Hufbauer (1968), Adler and Stevens (1974), Bergsten, Horst and Moran (1978), Horst (1974, 1976), Kindleberger (1969), Kravis and Lipsey (1982), Lipsey, Merle and Weiss (1976, 1981, 1984), Mansfield, Teece and Romeo (1979), Musgrave (1975), Stobough (1972, 1976), Vernon (1971, 1977), Young, Charles and Steigerwald (1990), Lipsey (1991). Germany: Bailey (1979), Donges and Juhl (1979), Fickentscher and Moritz (1980), Juhl (1984), Olle (1983). Others: Buckley and Arthisien (1986, international), Niehans (1977, Switzerland), Reddaway (1967, UK), Greenaway (1993, European Community), Chung (1990, Japan).

[34] For example: Ethier and Svensson (1986), Frankel (1965), Helpman (1984), Horstmann and Markusen (1989), Jasay (1960), Kemp (1962), Koizumi and Kopetzky (1988), Kojima (1982), Kojima and Ozawa (1984), MacDougall (1960; the "classic"), Markusen (1983), Mundell (1957), Neal and Pass (1990), Ruffin (1990), Wong (1986), Casson and Pearce (1986), Caves (1971, 1982), Hood and Young (1979).

[35] Rubner (1990) gives an example of the location of a GM components factory in the vicinity of Vienna: "In 1978 GM had global sales of more than $ 63 billion while in the same period little Austria's GDP was only $ 56 billion. Let the faithful draw their conclusions! A group of Austrian left-wingers felt conscience-bound to warn their fellow citizens that if GM were allowed to proceed with its nefarious project, this would be the first step in the subjugation of Austria by United States multis." (p. 35) Other examples could be cited. It is, however, not justified to expect this kind of effects. Counterexamples for an important strategic role of foreign subsidiaries for the whole group is the world competence of Siemens Austria for video-recorders or the reported extension of the production of SKF (Standard, 25. 3. 1993, p. 21) in Austria.

and domestic equity has a long tradition.[36] The policy debate hinges on the fact that Austria could face extortion from foreign firms threatening to relocate their subsidiaries. Despite some ideological arguments, the modern view of this issue is that ownership should not be overemphasized, and a mixed ownership structure is advantageous. As with the macrointegration effects, we do not go into detail on the political economy. The interested reader is asked to consult the literature cited.

Economic Effects

Economic theory analyzes effects of FDI on different levels. At the macro level, trade theory and the macro-type marginal-productivity theory assess effects on trade, capital flow, knowledge and the resulting income distribution. Since modern theory is more micro-based, it is increasingly applicable to FDI, because it takes the special features of FDI (being more often a package of tangible and intangible assets rather than a capital flow) into account, while orthodox trade theory did not. On the micro level, several models exist on the effects of FDI on exports in different markets (substituting or complementing exports), as well as the internalization of intermediate product markets. Two caveats should be made: first, theory does not allow us to make definite a priori suggestions about effects of FDI; and second, most models are partial models analyzing only few parameters involved.

Effects of FDI are usually defined by the difference, comparing the actual outcome with what would have been if the FDI would not have been carried out (that is, the counterfactual hypothesis).

Whereas so far most Austrian investment abroad was of a complementary nature (for example, sales subsidiaries, assembling), EC 92 promotes export-substituting FDI in the Union. For example, in the case of United States subsidiaries in the Union, Dunning (1991) argued that barriers to entry "are likely to favor the substitution of exports for local production". Along with the single-market inducement of FDI, the small firm size as well as the increasing number of production units abroad points to a sub-

---

[36] Wilkins (1970: 70) reports that it was the Austrian foreign minister who warned of the *défi américaine* already around 1900. For a recent discussion see Teufelsbauer (1989; a critique by Bellak (1992b) and a reply by Teufelsbauer (1992). See also Beirat für Wirtschafts- und Sozialfragen (1989).

stitutive relationship of FDI and exports. On the other hand, the increasing number and value of acquisitions abroad favors a complementary effect of FDI on exports. This is true at least in larger firms, which are responsible for the major share of FDI.

Determinants of Effects

The various effects depend, *inter alia*, on several factors.

- *The stage of internationalization of an economy.* The attitude towards an effect may change with an increasing amount of FDI. For example, internationalizing R&D to a certain extent may result in the acquisition of foreign know-how, but internationalizing the main parts of R&D may mean a loss of human capital and know how for the home country.
- *The level of development of the host country compared with the home country* points to certain types of FDI. A relatively less developed labor-abundant country will attract only the labor-intensive activities of firms from a highly developed country; a similar level of development of home and host countries will favor intraindustry FDI etc. If the degree of capacity utilization is already low, relocation may cause recession; if it is high, relocation may free resources for better use (for example, Japanese firms investing in NICs). Without knowing about the type and purpose of FDI, effects cannot be determined.[37] For example, capital transfer for loss coverage may not imply trade effects, whereas an assembly unit abroad does. Transferring know-how into FDI may mean a weakening of the competitiveness of the parent company and a strengthening of the subsidiary. Relocating headquarter services abroad may lead to a loss of value added etc.

Apart from these obvious determinants several firm-specific factors (for example, the organizational structure, the dependence of subsidiaries, transfer pricing and the subsidiaries' share of intermediate products in value-added obtained from the mother company) must be taken into account.

---

[37] For example, Cantwell (1993) discusses the relationship between international trade and various types of FDI.

Type of effects

Most studies concentrate on balance-of-payments and employment effects and, from these effects, other parameters are derived. Some studies mention a "house-cleaning effect" (Ozawa 1992), assessing the effects of relocation of activities on domestic investment and firm structure. Only a few studies can be found on the distributional consequences of FDI, on business-cycle effects or on effects of FDI on comparative or competitive advantages (Dunning and Gittelmann 1992; Dunning 1993).

Dimensions of effects

The various partial effects must be categorized by their dimension: direct and indirect (that is, effects in related industries) must be distinguished to differentiate first and second order effects. The type of FDI (for example, resource seeking, strategic asset-seeking), especially intangible FDI, implies effects on different parameters in the home country. Hence macroeconomic models assuming homogeneous FDI are not useful in this case (see above). Short, medium and long term have to be separated – the partial models often allow estimates only for the short run.

We now turn to the few empirical estimates available on effects of outward FDI, as well as of inward FDI, on the Austrian economy.

Effects of Outward FDI [38]

The effect of FDI on the balance of payments shows fluctuations in various years. The relatively small amount of directly outgoing capital for FDI[39] results in a small direct effect; adding export earnings (see below), the total balance-of-payments effect may be slightly positive.

Pichl (1990a, b) estimated in the "most likely realistic scenario" a direct net export-stimulating effect of ATS 10-12 billion p.a., that is, about 3-4% of exports of the manufacturing sector in 1988. From a time-series analysis, Pfaffermaier (1992, 1993) concluded that results pointed to a positive correlation of Austrian FDI and exports between industries. In other words, Austrian FDI and exports were found to have a complementary

[38] The lack of reliable data on intra-firm trade is a serious shortcoming for the following estimates. The estimates for 1988 are not representative for the whole period 1987-1992, because the substitution effects are likely to have increased as certainly has the capital involved.
[39] Part of it is used to cover losses, and not for real investment. According to the Central Bank, total earnings of FDI were negative throughout the years.

relationship. The dominance of sales subsidiaries (Bellak and Weiss 1992) over production units abroad supports the argument.

Several authors have argued that gross domestic investment and FDI are complementary in the case of SMOPECs (Oxelheim and Braunerhjelm 1992), dominated by a small number of large multinational firms. Walsh (1988) supported this argument: "small countries... tend to have relatively fewer firms with the economic and commercial capacity to be successful in international markets."

Belderbos (1992) provided evidence of the existence of a degree of interdependence between domestic investment and FDI. He concluded that domestic and foreign investment are "substitutory in character" and domestic investment depends at part on the "profitability and demand differentials between the home market and foreign locations". Unfortunately, no estimates are available on the relationship between domestic and foreign investment for Austria.

The estimate of the resulting domestic employment effect of 11,000-14,000 additional employees (that is, 2.0-2.6% of employment in the manufacturing sector) is based on the export-stimulus effect and includes direct as well as indirect effects.

Concerning the competitiveness of firms, the R&D expenditure of firms with production units abroad (ATS 48,400) was relatively higher than those without (ATS 31,500) in 1988. If one accepts R&D as a competitiveness indicator, this might indicate competitive advantages (ownership advantages) exploited via FDI; yet so far the causal relationship between R&D and FDI has not been tested for Austria.

Effects of Inward FDI

The only large-scale survey on effects of foreign investment in Austria was conducted by Glatz and Moser (1989a, b). They examined all large investments (36) in the manufacturing sector since 1970, which were attracted by the state agency ICD (Industrial Corporate Development) and received subsidies. In contrast to Pichl, the figures did not give the effect (that is, the balance of the real and the counterfactual situation), but the real development. For this purpose indicators for foreign subsidiaries in Austria were compared with the Austrian average.

Growth and employment effects of foreign subsidiaries in Austria were higher than in Austrian firms. The annual average employment growth 1980 and 1986 was +7.7% for the former; -1.9% for the latter. The investment-turnover ratio was also significantly higher in the former (10.6%) than in the latter group.[40] The balance-of-payments effect, in particular the direct effect on the trade balance, was positive because of the high export ratio of foreign subsidiaries (85%). It may have been, however, reduced if the share of imported intermediate services (75%) had been taken into account. Glatz and Moser stated that, in the long run, capital outflow will exceed capital inflows.

The value-added effect is highly positive, the value added per employee in foreign subsidiaries being 25% above the average of the Austrian manufacturing sector. The higher efficiency may be an effect of a few, highly specialized activities of foreign subsidiaries, some of them being only assembly lines.

An important question for a small home country is whether technology is transferred and R&D conducted in the subsidiary of the foreign firms. This issue is regarded as favorable in the case of Austria, since foreign firms transferred foreign know-how into their subsidiaries, and their R&D ratio (5.12% in 1986) was more than twice as high as the manufacturing total. However the effect on the Austrian economy has been small since know-how has been used primarily intrafirm, and there might have been some transfer of human capital abroad.

The (vertical and horizontal) relationship of foreign subsidiaries with Austrian firms is seen as problematic, since there is only one additional job created per three employees in a foreign subsidiary in Austria. State subsidies to attract foreign firms are thus not as efficient as they could have been. Overall, Glatz and Moser concluded that the quantitative effects (like employment, investment volume) outweighed the qualitative effects (like upgrading, linkages to Austrian firms, structural impacts etc.) of foreign subsidiaries and that subsidization should have been more oriented toward the latter.

IV. Conclusions

In general, we conclude that microintegration (defined as trade and FDI with barriers) is a necessary tool for fully and quickly utilizing the integration potential of macrointegration (that is, without barriers). From the

---

[40] The comparison of foreign subsidiaries and domestic firms is problematic because the firm structure (range of activities etc.) might be totally different.

theoretical discussion above, as well as from the empirical results, it follows that the more microintegrated a small-country firm has been prior to macrointegration, the more advantageous the effects of macrointegration will be. These firms will have substantially lower adaptation costs and already have some experience in the integrated market. Existing FDI may be more quickly relocated or restructured than FDI starting from scratch. More crudely put, a low degree of microintegration for a small country would imply that larger countries (and hence larger firms) would gain relatively more.

Austria's outsider response via FDI is a step towards reducing this integration gap. The chance to reap additional effects of macrointegration rises with increasing FDI in the single market. A survey by Pichl (1989c) revealed that 63% of Austrian manufacturing firms expected intensified competition regardless of Austrian Union membership, yet the share of firms that had already established production units in the Union was somewhat lower. In addition, 59% of respondents to the Austrian Technology and Innovation Survey 1990 said they exploited their competitive advantages abroad (Leo, Palme and Volk 1992), and 72% said they would do so in the near future.

Austrian firms in the exposed sector with high export ratios and/or large FDI abroad will have few incentives from macrointegration to restructure their activities. The majority of sheltered-sector firms probably underestimated the restructuring requirements and will be seriously affected by macrointegration. Thus, in sheltered sectors as well as in sectors hit by competitive pressure from eastern Europe, there will be conflict between the micro- and macrointegration strategies – while we can expect harmony in the open sector.

References

Acoccella, N. (1990): The Multinational Firm and the Theory of Industrial Organization. In B. Dankbaar, J. Groenewegen, H. Schenk (eds.) *Perspectives in Industrial Organization*, Dordrecht: Kluwer Academic Publishers: 233-51.

Adler, M. and V. G. G. Stevens (1974): The Trade Effects of Direct Investment, *Journal of Finance 29*(2): 655-76.

Adler, M. and C. G. Hufbauer (1968): Overseas Manufacturing Investment and the Balance of Payments, United States Department GPO, Washington, DC: *Tax Policy Research Study* No. I.

Andersson, J. O. (1990): *The 1992 Project From A Small Country Perspective*, Stockholm: IUI. *IUI Working Paper*, No. 280.

Arbeiterkammer (ed.) (1989): Fusionen und Übernahmen. *Informationen über Multinationale Konzerne*, Sondernummer.

Bach, W. (1992): Die Situation Österreichs bei Direktinvestitionen, *Informationen über Multinationale Konzerne* No. 2: 10-12.

Bailey, P. J. (1979): *Employment Effects of Multinational Enterprises: A Survey of Relevant Studies relating to the Federal Republic of Germany*. Geneva: ILO (Working Paper No. 2).

Baldwin, R. E. (1992): Measurable Dynamic Gains from Trade. *Journal of Political Economy 100*: 162-74.

Bayer, K. (1991): EG Binnenmarkt und Wettbewerbsstärke der österreichischen Sachgütererzeugung, *WIFO Monatsberichte* 8: 484-91.

Bayer, K. (1992): Austria. In EFTA (ed.) *Effects of "1992" on the Manufacturing industries of the EFTA Countries*. Geneva (EFTA): 59-113. (*EFTA Occasional Papers*, No. 38).

Bayer, K. and G. Wetzel (1992): Neuere Entwicklungen auf dem österreichischen Markt für Unternehmensfusionen, *WIFO Monatsberichte* 7: 387-95.

Beer, E., B. Ederer, W. Goldmann, R. Lang, M. Passweg and R. Reitzner (1991): *Wem gehört Österreichs Wirtschaft wirklich?* Vienna: Orac.

Beirat für Wirtschafts- und Sozialfragen (ed.) (1992): *Internationalisierung*. Vienna.

Belderbos, R. A. (1992): Large Multinational Enterprises Based in a Small Economy: Effects on Domestic Investment. *Review of World Economics 128* (3): 543-47.

Bellak, C. (1992a): Die Entwicklung der österreichischen Direktinvestitionen in Österreich von 1980-1990. In IWI (ed.) *Series Internationalization*. Vol. VI. Vienna: Austria Press: 17-73.

Bellak, C. (1992b): Zu einer verfügungsrechtsorientierten Strukturpolitik, *Wirtschaftspolitische Blätter* 3: 369-83.

Bellak, C. (1992): *Outsider's Response to Europe 1992: Case of Austria. Working Paper of the University of Economics*. No. 16, Vienna: University of Economics.

Bellak, C. (1992): *Vorbild oder Warnung?* Vienna: University of Economics (mimeo).

Bellak, C. (1993): *Effekte aktiver Direktinvestitionen im Ursprungsland.* Vienna: Peter Lang.

Bellak, C. (1994): Outsiders' Response to EC'92 – Evidence from Austria, *Multinational Business Review*. Vol. 2, No. 1: 40-3.

Bellak, C., O. Fischer, P. Podesser and P. Schönhofer (1989): Die Internationalisierung der österreichischen Industrie – Eine Standortbestimmung. In IWI (ed.) *Series Internationalization*. Vol. I. Vienna: RM-Verlag.

Bellak, C. and R. Luostarinen (1994): *Foreign Direct Investment of Small and Open Economies: Case of Austria and Finland. CIBR-Report X-1.* Helsinki: School of Economics.

Bellak, C. and M. Oettl (1990): Die internationale Präsenz der österreichischen Industrie – Die Kernaussagen der IWI Untersuchung., In: IWI (ed.) *Series Internationalization*. Vol. IV. Vienna: Austria Press.

Bellak, C. and A. Weiss (1992): *The Competitive Advantage of Austria.* Copenhagen: Business and Economic Studies on European Integration, *DSRI Working Paper* 18.

Bellak, C. and A. Weiss (1993): The Austrian Diamond. *Management International Review*. Special Issue (2): 109-18.

Bergsten, C. F., T. Horst and T. H. Moran (1978): *American Multinationals and American Interests.* Washington, DC: The Brookings Institution.

Borner, S. (ed.) (1980): *Produktionsverlagerung und industrieller Strukturwandel.* Bern: Paul Haupt.

Borner, S. (1986a): Neue Formen der Internationalisierung aus der Sicht einer kleinen offenen Volkswirtschaft: Konsequenzen für Unternehmensstrategien und Wirtschaftspolitik. In Aiginger K., Schriftenreihe der Investkredit AG (ed.) *Weltwirtschaft und unternehmerische Strategien*, Vol. 13. Vienna: Investkredit AG: 45-52.

Borner, S. (1986b): *Internationalization of Industry – An Assessment in the Light of a Small Open Economy (Switzerland)*. Berlin: Springer.

Breuss, F. (1983): *Österreichs Außenwirtschaft 1945-1982*. Vienna: Signum.

Breuss, F. (1992): Statische und dynamische Effekte der bisherigen Europa-Integration Österreichs. Vienna: WIFO, WIFO Working Papers, (50).

Breuss, F., H. Handler and J. Stankovsky (1988): *Österreichische Optionen einer EG-Annäherung und ihre Folgen*. Vienna: WIFO.

Breuss, F. and J. Stankovsky (1988): *Österreich und der EG-Binnenmarkt*. Vienna: Signum.

Breuss, F., H. Handler and J. Stankovsky (1989): Economic Relations with the EC - The Austrian View. In *Svensk industri inför EG '92*. Stockholm: SIND (2): 35-50.

Breuss, F. and E. Kitzmantel (ed.) (1993): Die Europäische Integration: Untersuchung der sektoralen Auswirkungen auf Österreich. In: *Schriftenreihe Integrationsinformation*, Band 1. Vienna: BMF.

Breuss, F. and F. Schebeck (1989): The Completion of EC's Internal Market and its Impact on the Austrian Economy, Macroeconomic Model Simulations. Vienna: *WIFO Working Papers* (31).

Breuss, F. and F. Schebeck (1991): *Der EG-Binnenmarkt und Österreich, Sensitivitätsanalysen mit dem WIFO-Makromodell*. Vienna: WIFO.

Breuss, F. and F. Schebeck (1991): Österreich im EWR. *WIFO-Monatsberichte 64* (5): 285-90.

Buckley, P. and P. Arthisien (1986): *Die Multinationalen Unternehmen und der Arbeitsmarkt. IRM Dossiers*. Geneva: Campus.

Buigues, P. and F. Ilzkovitz (1989): *The Sectoral Impact of the Internal Market*. EC-Doc II/335/88-EN. Luxembourg: Commission of the European Communities.

Cantwell, J. (1992): The Effects of Integration on the Structure of MNC Activity in the EC. In M. W. Klein and P. J.J. Welfens (eds.) *Multinationals in Europe and Global Trade in the 1990s*. Berlin: Springer Verlag: 193-233.

Cantwell, J. (1993): *The Relationship Between International Trade and International Production*. Reading: University of Reading: (mimeo).

Casson, M. and R. D. Pearce (1986): *The Welfare Effects of Foreign Enterprise, A Diagrammatic Analysis, University of Reading Discussion Papers in International Investment and Business Studies, No. 98, October*, University of Reading: Reading

Caves, R. E. (1971): Multinational Corporations: The Industrial Economics of Foreign Investment. *Economica*, Vol. XXXVIII: 1-27.

Caves, R. E. (1982): *Multinational Enterprise and Economic Analysis*. Cambridge: Cambridge University Press.

Chung, H. L. (1990): Outward direct foreign investment and structural adjustment in a small open economy. *Kobe Economic Business Review 36*: 1-15.

Dockner, E. and A. Sitz (1986): An Investigation into Austrian Export Pricing: Price Taking or Price Setting of a Small Open Economy? *Empirica 13* (2): 221-41.

Donges, J. B. and P. Juhl (1979): Deutsche Privatinvestitionen im Ausland: Export von Arbeitsplätzen? *Konjunkturpolitik*. *25* (4): 203-24.

Dunning, J. H. (1981): Explaining the International Direct Investment Position of Countries: Towards a Dynamic or Developmental Approach, *Review of World Economics 117* (1): 30-64.

Dunning, J. H. (1991): *European Integration and Transatlantic Foreign Direct Investment: The Record Assessed. DSRI Working Paper 3*. Copenhagen: Copenhagen Business School.

Dunning, J. H. (1993): MNEs, Technology and Innovatory Capacity: A Home Country Perspective. In *Multinational Enterprises and the Global Economy*. Wokingham: Addison-Wesley: 331-48.

Dunning, J. H. and M. Gittelmann (1992): Japanese Multinationals in Europe and the United States: Exporting Cars, Computers, and Comparative Advantage through Foreign Direct Investment. In P.J.J. Welfens (ed.) *Multinationals in Europe and Global Trade*. Berlin: Springer.

Dunning, J. H. and P. Robson (eds.) (1988): *Multinationals and the European Community*. Oxford, Basil Blackwell.

Eliasson, G. and L. Lundberg (1989): *The Creation of the EC Internal Market and its Effects on the Competitiveness of Producers in other Industrial Economies. IUI Working Paper* No. 229. Stockholm: IUI.

Erbe, S., H. Großmann, R. Jungnickel, G. Koopmann and H.-E. Scharrer (1991): *Drittlandunternehmen im europäischen Binnenmarkt: Zwischen Liberalismus und Protektionismus*. Hamburg: Verlag Weltarchiv GmbH.

Ethier, W. J. and L. E.O. Svensson (1986): The Theorems Of International Trade With Factor Mobility. *Journal of International Economics 20*: 21-42.

Felderer, B. (1974): Thesen zu ökonomischen Problemen kleiner Volkswirtschaften, *Jahrbuch für Sozialwissenschaften 25*: 106-14.

Fickentscher, W. R. and P. Moritz (1980): *Die Auswirkungen deutscher Direktinvestitionen in Entwicklungsländern auf Produktion und Beschäftigung in der Bundesrepublik Deutschland*. Tübingen: J.C.B. Mohr.

Frankel, M. (1965): Home Versus Foreign Investment: A Case Against Capital Exports. *Kyklos 17*: 411-33.

Glatz, H. and H. Moser (1989a): Ausländische Direktinvestitionen und Industriepolitik, *Wirtschaft und Gesellschaft* Vol. 15, No. 1. Vienna: 33-61.

Glatz, H. and H. Moser (1989b): *Auswirkungen ausländischer Direktinvestiionen in der österreichischen Industrie*. Vienna: Campus.

Goldmann, W. (1991): Deutsche Direktinvestitionen im Ausland und österreichische Direktinvestitionen in der BRD. In *Informationen über Multinationale Konzerne*. Vienna: Arbeiterkammer.

Graham, E. M. (1992): Direct Investment between the United States and the European Community Post-1986 and Pre-1992. In J. Cantwell (ed.) *Multinational Investment in Modern Europe*. Aldershot: Eward Elgar: 46-70.

Greenaway, D. (1993): Handel und ausländische Direktinvestitionen. In Commission of the European Communities (ed.) Die EG als Welthandelspartner. *European Economy 52*: 115-42.

Guger, A. (1992): Lohnstückkostenposition der Industrie 1991 verbessert. *WIFO Monatsberichte 7*: 381-86.

Guger, A., W. Pollan and M. Wüger (1990): Auswirkungen einer EG-Mitgliedschaft Österreichs auf Preise und Kosten. Vienna: WIFO, *WIFO Gutachten*.

Heitger, B. and J. Stehn (1990): Japanese Direct Investments in the EC – Response to the Internal Market 1993? *Journal of Common Market Studies 29* (1): 1-15.

Hellmer, S. (1988): *Kleine, offene Volkswirtschaften und die europäische Integration – eine sozioökonomische Strukturanalyse*. Vienna: Ludwig Boltzmann Institut.

Helpman, E. (1984): A Simple Theory of International Trade with Multinational Corporations, *Journal of Political Economy 92* (3): 451-71.

Hirsch, S. and T. Almor (1992): *Outsiders' Response to Europe 1992: Theoretical Considerations and Empirical Evidence. DSRI Working Paper 9*. Copenhagen: Copenhagen Business School.

Hood, N. and S. Young (1979): *The economics of multinational enterprise*. New York: Longman.

Horst, T. (1974): *American Exports and Foreign Direct Investments*. Cambridge, MA: Harvard Institute of Economic Research. (*Discussion Paper*, No. 376).

Horst, T. (1976): American Multinationals and the U.S. Economy. *American Economic Review*, Vol. 66, May: 149-54.

Horstmann, I. J. and J. R. Markusen (1989): Firm Specific Assets and the Gains from Direct Foreign Investment. *Economica 56*: 41-48.

IWI (ed.) (1990): *Foreign Direct Investment by Austrian Manufacturers. A Survey*. Vienna: Austria Press.

Jasay, A.E. (1960): The Social Choice Between Home and Overseas Investment, *Economic Journal 70*: 105-13.

Juhl, P. (1984): Ergebnisse neuerer Untersuchungen der heimischen Beschäftigungseffekte von Auslandsinvestitionen, *World Economic Review 120* (2): 376-84.

Kemp, M. C. (1962): The Benefits and Costs of Private Investment from Abroad: Comment, *Economic Record 38*: 108-10.

Kindleberger, C. P. (1969): *American Business Abroad: Six Lectures on Direct Investment*. New Haven: Yale University Press.

Koizumi, T. and K. J. Kopetzky (1988): Foreign Direct Investment, Technology Transfer and Domestic Employment Effects. *Journal of International Economics 10*: 1-20.

Kojima, K. (1982): Macroeconomic versus International Business Approach to Direct Foreign Investment. *Hitotsubashi Journal of Economics 23* (1): 1-19.

Kojima, K. and T. Ozawa (1984): Micro- and Macro-Economic Models of Direct Foreign Investment: Toward a Synthesis. *Hitotsubashi Journal of Economics 25*: 1-20.

Kramer, H. (1991): Imperfections in European Economic Integration. Observations from an Austrian Viewpoint. In EFTA (ed.) *EFTA Countries in a Changing Europe*. 30th Anniversary Round Table. Geneva: EFTA, 25-39.

Kravis, I. B. and R. E. Lipsey (1982): The Location of Overseas Production and Production for Export by U.S. Multinational Firms. *Journal of International Economics 12*: 201-23.

Leo, H., G. Palme and E. Volk (1992): Die Innovationstätigkeit der österreichischen Industrie. In: *Technologie und Innovationstest 1990*. Vienna: WIFO.

Lipsey, R. (1991): *Foreign direct investment in the US and US Trade. NBER Working Paper*, No. 3623. Cambridge MA: National Bureau of Economic Research.

Lipsey, R. E. and M. Y. Weiss (1976): *Exports and Foreign Investment in Manufacturing Industries. NBER Working Paper*, No. 131 (rev. ed.). New York: National Bureau of Economic Research.

Lipsey, R., E. Merle and Y. Weiss (1981): Foreign Production and Exports in Manufacturing Industries. *Review of Economics and Statistics 163*: 488-94.

Lipsey, R., E. Merle and Y. Weiss (1984): Foreign Production and Exports of Individual Firms. *Review of Economics and Statistics 62* (2): 304-8.

Luostarinen, R. (1980): *Internationalization of the Firm*. Helsinki: HSE.

MacDougall, G.D.A. (1960): The Benefits and Costs of Private Investment from Abroad: A Theoretical Approach, *Economic Record 36*: 13-35.

Mansfield, E., D. J. Teece and A. Romeo (1979): Overseas Research and Development by US-Based Firms, *Economica 46*, (May): 187-96.

Marin, D. (1983): *Wechselkurs und Industriegewinne*. Eine empirische Studie zu den Verteilungswirkungen der Währungspolitik in Österreich. Frankfurt: Campus Verlag.

Markusen, J. R. (1983): Factor Movements and Commodity Trade As Complements. *Journal of International Economics 14*: 341-56.

Mundell, R. A. (1957): International Trade and Factor Mobility. *American Economic Review 47*: 321-47.

Musgrave, P. (1975): *Direct Investment Abroad and the Multinationals: Effects on the United States Economy. Report prepared for the Subcommittee on Multinational Corporations of the Senate Foreign Relations Committee.* Washington, DC: US Government Printing Office.

Neal, B. and C. Pass (1990): Foreign Direct Investment: Potential Costs and Benefits for Host and Source Countries. *Management Accounting*: 32-34 and 49.

Niehans, J. (1977): *Benefits of Multinational Firms for a Small Economy: The Case of Switzerland.* In Agmon, T. and Kindleberger, C. P. (ed.) Multinationals from Small Countries. Cambridge: MIT Press: 1-39.

Olle, W. (1983): *Strukturveränderungen der internationalen Investitionen und inländischer Arbeitsmarkt.* München: Minerva Publikation.

Oxelheim, L. and P. Braunerhjelm (1992): *Heckscher-Ohlin and Schumpeter Industries: The Response by Swedish Multinational Firms to the EC 1992 Program. IUI Working Paper*, No. 352. Stockholm: IUI.

Ozawa, T. (1991): Japan in a New Phase of Multinationalism and Industrial Upgrading: Functional Integration of Trade, Growth and FDI, *Journal of World Trade 25* (1): 43-60.

Pfaffermeier, M. (1992): *Foreign Direct Investment and Exports: A Time Series Approach, Arbeitspapier.* No. 9212. Linz: University of Linz.

Pfaffermeier, M. (1993): *Foreign Outward Direct Investment and Exports of Austrian Industries. Mimeo.* Linz.

Pichl, C. (1989a): Direktinvestitionen und Beteiligungen im Ausland. *WIFO Monatsberichte 62* (6): 416-27.

Pichl, C. (1989b): Internationale Investitionen. *WIFO Monatsberichte 62* (3): 161-75.

Pichl, C. (1989c): Integrationseffekte aus der Sicht der österreichischen Industrieunternehmen, *WIFO-Monatsberichte 62* (1): 668-78.

Pichl, C. (1990a): *Volkswirtschaftliche Effekte einer aktiven Internationalisierung der Produktion.* Vienna: Unpublished.

Pichl, C. (1990b): Braucht Österreich eigene transnational tätige Unternehmen? *Informationen über Multinationale Konzerne 1:* 1-4.

Pichler, J.H. (Coordinator) (1992): *Ökonomische Konsequenzen eines EG-Beitritts Österreichs.* Projektstudie. Vienna: OeNB (Jubiläumsfonds-Projekt Nr. 3773).

Polt, W. (1992): *Technology Programmes in Small Open Economies, A Review of Recent Experiences. OEFZS-4662.* Seibersdorf: Österreichisches Forschung-Zentrum.

Proske, D. (1989): Direktinvestitionen im Ausland. *Economy 5:* 46-52.

Reddaway, N.B. (1967): *UK Direct Investment Overseas: Final Report.* University of Cambridge Department of Applied Economics, *Occasional Papers*, No. 12. London: Cambridge University Press.

Robinson, E.A.G. (ed.) (1960): *Economic Consequences of the Size of Nations.* London: MacMillan.

Rothschild, K. W. (1989): Ziele, Ereignisse und Reaktionen: Reflexionen über die österreichische Wirtschaftspolitik. In H. Abele, E. Nowotny, S. Schleicher and G. Winckler (eds.) *Handbuch der österreichischen Wirtschaftspolitik.* 3rd. edn. Vienna: Manz: 113-24.

Rubner, A. (1990): *The Might of the Multinationals*, New York: Praeger.

Ruffin, R. J. (1990): International Factor Movements. In R. Jones & P. Kenen (eds.) *Handbook of International Economics*. New York: North Holland: 237-88.

Rugman, A. M. and A. Verbeke (1991): Competitive Strategies for Non-European firms. In B. Bürgenmeier and J.L. Mucchielli (eds.) *Multinationals and Europe 1992*. London: Routledge: 22-35.

Schulmeister, S. (1990): Das technologische Profil des österreichischen Außenhandels, *WIFO Monatsberichte 63* (12): 663-75.

Senjur, M. (1992): The Viability of Economic Development of a Small State Seperating from a Larger One. *Development and International Cooperation 8* (14-15): 5-22.

Siegel, D. (1992): Die Bedeutung österreichischer multinationaler Konzerne für die Internationalisierung. In IWI (ed.) *Series Internationalization*. Vol. VI. Vienna: IWI: 165-89.

Siegel, D. (1993): *Multis made in Austria*. In IWI (ed.) Studies, Vol. IX, Vienna: IWI.

Stankovsky, J. (1992): Internationalisierung Österreichs in Osteuropa. In IWI (ed.) *Series Internationalization*. Vol. VI. Vienna: IWI: 223-36.

Steindl, J. (1977): Import and Production of Know-how in a Small Country: The Case of Austria. In C.T. Saunders (ed.) *Industrial Policy and Technology Transfer between East and West*. New York: Springer Verlag: 211-18.

Stobough, R. B. (1972): How investment abroad creates jobs at home. *Harvard Business Review 50*: 118-26.

Stobough, R. B. (1976): *Nine Investments Abroad and Their Impact at Home*. Boston: Harvard University Press.

Teufelsbauer, W. (1989): Zu einer verfügungsrechtsorientierten Strukturpolitik, *Wirtschaftspolitische Blätter,* Volume 36. (3): 274-89.

Teufelsbauer, W. (1992): Zu Bellaks Kritik einer verfügungsrechtsorientierten Strukturpolitik. *Wirtschaftspolitische Blätter,* Volume 39. (3): 384-92.

UNCTC (ed.) (1990): Regional Economic Integration and Transnational Corporations in the 1990s: Europe 1992, North America, and Developing Countries. *UNCTC Current Studies,* No. 15, July. New York: UNCTC.

Urban, W. (1989): Österreichische Auslandsinvestitionen – Rückblick und Ausblick, *Wirtschaftsanalysen*. Vienna: EÖSpC.

Vernon, R. (1971): *Souvereignty at Bay*. London: Basic Books.

Vernon, R. (1977): *Storm over the Multinationals. The real issues*. Cambridge: Harvard University Press.

Walsh, V. (1987): *Technology, Competitiveness and the Special Problem of Small Countries. STI Review 2*. Paris: OECD.

Walsh, V. (1988): Technology and the Competitiveness of Small Countries: Review. In C. Freeman and B.-A. Lundvall (eds.) *Small Countries Facing the Technological Revolution*. London: Pinter Publishers: 36-66.

Wieser, T. (1989): *Price Differentials in the European Economic Space (EES). EFTA Occasional Papers*, No. 29. Geneva: EFTA.

Wilkins, M. (1970): *The Emergence of Multinational Enterprise: American Business Abroad from the Colonial Era to 1914*. Cambridge, MA: Harvard University Press.

Winckler, G. (1989): Die Schaffung des EG-Binnenmarktes und seine Folgen für Österreich: eine wirtschaftspolitische Analyse. *ÖZP 3*: 223-30.

Wong, K.-Y. (1986): Are International Trade and Factor Mobility Substitutes? *Journal of International Economics 21*: 25-43.

Yannopoulos, G. N. (1992): Multinational Corporations and the Single European Market. In J. Cantwell (ed.) *Multinational Investment in Modern Europe*. Aldershot: Eward Elgar: 329-48.

Young, K., H. Charles and E. Steigerwald, (1990): Is Foreign Investment in the U.S. Transferring U.S. Technology Abroad? *Business Economics 25* (4): 28-30.

Chapter 4:
Structural Implications of the Investment Response by Swedish Multinational Firms to the EC 1992 Program

Pontus Braunerhjelm and Lars Oxelheim

The locational decisions of firms hinge on a mixture of purely firm-specific factors and country-based or institutional considerations of a more general character. For instance, the adoption of global strategies, the need to attain a competitive position in markets, differences in relative costs and institutional settings across markets all influence the choice of production sites. An increasingly important factor in that respect is the design of economic policy within regions and countries. As policy-makers have begun to realize the political pay-offs of attracting inward investments, the risk of countries becoming involved in a global race for investment has increased (Oxelheim 1993). Depending on the structure and extent of that race, losers or latecomers could find themselves in a situation of permanent lower growth.

Of particular interest during the 1980s was the institutional wedge created between insiders and outsiders by European integration. The massive inflow of foreign direct investment (FDI) in the European Union in the late 1980s and early 1990s, suggests that firms expected the beneficial effects of the internal market to accrue predominantly to insiders. Evidence has also been forwarded that fear of being excluded from a potential growth market was a major determinant of the inflows of investments from outsider firms – European as well as American and Japanese – into the Common Market (Braunerhjelm 1990, Karlsen 1990, Yamawaki 1990, Yannopoulous 1990, 1992, Ozawa 1992, Rugman and Verbeke 1991, US International Trade Commission 1992).

The purpose of this chapter is to shed light on the impact of the EC 1992 program, launched in the mid 1980s, on the distribution of Swedish FDI across industries and regions. Sweden may be of special interest as it is often claimed to have one of the most multinational industries in the world (Andersson and Fredriksson 1993). Moreover, Sweden is one of very few industrial countries for which cross-tabulated data on FDI by sectors and countries are accessible. Hence, to what extent did the implementation of integration policies within the Union from 1985 and onwards influence the distribution of Swedish investment across regions? Did it divert investment away from Sweden or did the expected positive effects of the EC 1992 spill over to create indigenous investment opportunities as well? If so, can we detect different patterns with regard to the allocation of investment in knowledge-oriented industries or in more basically oriented industries? Furthermore, does foreign investment substitute or complement domestic investment, and can we observe any significant differences across industries? The answers to these questions largely determine the future potential for industrial production in Sweden and carry important policy implications.

The theoretical foundation of this chapter rests on the eclectic framework developed by Dunning (1977). Regression analysis will be used to study the response by firms to the EC 1992 program. In particular, we estimate the interdependence between foreign and domestic investment. We also attempt to examine to what extent the increased foreign operations of Swedish firms in the 1980s can be attributed to factors pertaining to the Swedish economy. The data set used in the analysis covers the regional distribution of investment by Swedish industries in the manufacturing sector during the period 1982-1992.[41]

The rest of the chapter is organized as follows. In Section II, the pattern and characteristics of Swedish FDI are outlined. Thereafter, the theoretical rationale for engaging in foreign operations is presented in Section III. The hypotheses that we will test through regression analyses are presented in Section IV, and Section V contains the definitions of the industries, the data set and the empirical results. The main conclusions are summarized in Section VI.

I. Background

Sweden has pursued a free trade oriented policy for a long time. Over 50% of Sweden's international exchange of goods and services takes place with

---

[41] For a description of the definition of FDI applied in this article and the problems encountered in the measurement process, see Appendix I in Chapter 2.

Figure 22. Swedish foreign direct investment (FDI), total and in the European Community, 1982-1992: deflated by the GDP implicit price index (1984 = 100), annual data.

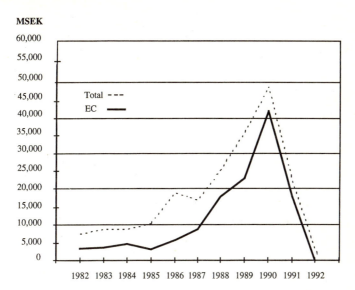

Sources: Based on data from the Swedish central bank (FDI) and Statistics Sweden (implicit price index).

the Union, followed by the United States as the second most important recipient of Swedish commodities. For some industries, notably the car industry, the United States market is of core importance.

The Swedish manufacturing industry is dominated by relatively few, large multinational firms, with a long tradition of production abroad. A shift in the regional distribution of their investment could therefore be expected to carry macroeconomic repercussions. The dependence of Swedish firms on the nearby European market implies that differences in the institutional setting between the two markets, as represented by the EC 1992 program, could be expected to influence the behavior of Swedish firms (Buigues and Jacquemin 1989; Burgenmeier and Mucchielli 1991; Hirsch and Meshulach 1992).

Figure 22 shows the overall picture of the evolution of Swedish FDI in the period 1982-1992 and the distribution between the Union and the rest of the world. It gives a first indication of the impact on investment flows of the decision to create the internal market. In that period the real stock

Figure 23. Accumulated Swedish foreign direct investment (FDI) in the European Community and the United States, 1982-92: deflated by the GDP implicit price index (1984 = 100), annual data.

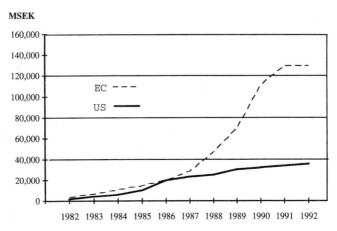

Sources: Based on data from the Swedish central bank (FDI) and Statistics Sweden (implicit price index).

of Swedish FDI in the Union increased by an average annual rate of about 45%. From an accumulated flow of SEK 22 billion for the period 1984-1987 investment increased to SEK 101 billion for 1988-1992.

Looking at each separate year in Figure 22, FDI peaked in 1990, and then it fell quite dramatically in 1991 and 1992. Swedish FDI shifted towards the Union after 1987. In the period 1982-1986, as shown in Figure 23, FDI in the United States and the Union followed almost identical paths, both with respect to the rate of change and the amounts invested. From 1987, the growth of Swedish FDI in the Union has been spectacular, whereas FDI in the United States remains more or less constant. Obviously, the high degree of internationalization of Swedish firms did not prevent them from building up further capacity abroad in the 1980s. A suggested explanation is that the firms reacted to the EC 1992 program by concentrating investment in Europe.

To examine the structural implications of increased foreign investment, the manufacturing sector has been divided into knowledge-intensive industry and more basically-oriented industry. Firms in the latter type of industry base their competitiveness on country-specific resources. Econo-

Table 14. Swedish total foreign investment in Schumpeter-industries and Heck-scher-Ohlin-industries, 1982-1992: net investment, millions of SEK.

Year	Current prices flows		Real (1984 prices) flows		Real (1984 prices) accumulated	
	S-products	H-products	S-products	H-products	S-products	H-products
1982	2,833	987	3,369	1,174	3,369	1,174
1983	4,335	1,159	4,677	1,251	8,046	2,424
1984	4,148	752	4,148	752	12,194	3,176
1985	3,970	457	3,717	428	15,911	3,604
1986	13,502	840	12,688	735	28,599	4,339
1987	9,377	1,547	7,814	1,289	36,413	5,628
1988	11,587	4,514	9,059	3,529	45,473	9,157
1989	11,680	6,184	8,439	4,468	53,912	13,626
1990	13,140	23,709	8,719	15,733	62,631	29,358
1991	19,013	380	11,744	235	74,376	29,593
1992	-3,390	-4,651	-2,061	-2,827	72,315	26,766

Note: Schumpeter (S) denotes knowledge-intensive industries, and Heckscher-Ohlin (H) refers to basic industries.

Sources: Based on data from the Swedish central bank (FDI) and Statistics Sweden (implicit price index).

mies of scale appear on the plant level, implying that production is concentrated in a limited number of units (Braunerhjelm 1990). Henceforth, they will be referred to as Heckscher-Ohlin firms or, if aggregated, the Heckscher-Ohlin industry. These firms are associated with the traditional trade framework, where factors are immobile between countries.

In knowledge-intensive industries the competitiveness of firms is built on individual, firm-specific knowledge. A conspicuous feature of production in these industries is the role assigned to R&D and other headquarters services. This allows economies of scale to be derived on the firm level, that is, even though production is spread on many units, they all benefit from some common, non-rivalry, firm-specific input. The firms belonging to this category are called Schumpeter firms or, if aggregated, the

Table 15. Swedish foreign direct investment in the EC in Schumpeter-industries and Heckscher-Ohlin-industries, 1982-1992: net investment, millions of SEK.

Year	Current prices flows		Real (1984 prices) flows		Real (1984 prices) accumulated	
	S-products	H-products	S-products	H-products	S-products	H-products
1982	1,298	502	1,543	597	1,543	597
1983	2,139	143	2,308	154	3,851	751
1984	2,453	189	2,453	189	6,304	940
1985	1,601	300	1,499	281	7,803	1,221
1986	3,496	420	3,059	367	10,862	1,589
1987	4,615	1,399	3,846	1,166	14,708	2,754
1988	7,377	4,192	5,768	3,278	20,476	6,032
1989	6,883	5,773	4,973	4,171	25,449	10,203
1990	9,941	22,906	6,597	15,200	32,045	25,403
1991	20,433	503	12,622	311	44,667	25,714
1992	-4,842	-4,772	-2,943	-2,901	41,724	22,813

Note: Schumpeter (S) denotes knowledge-intensive industries, and Heckscher-Ohlin (H) refers to basic industries.

Sources: See Table 14.

Schumpeter industry. Hence, the main difference between the two types of firms or industries refers to the sources of competitiveness, that is, proprietary firm-specific assets or country-fixed resources.[42]

As is obvious from Tables 14 and 15, investment followed different paths in the two industries during the 1980s. In 1992, the stock of Schumpeter firms' investment into the EC was almost twice times the size of the Heckscher-Ohlin firms' investment. FDI by the Schumpeter industry increased in 1986 to a new level. The Heckscher-Ohlin industry's FDI shifted upward dramatically in 1990, the only year FDI in the Heckscher-Ohlin industry exceeded FDI by the Schumpeter industry. This shift can, however, be pinpointed to two major takeovers by Swedish firms in the forest industry.[43]

---

[42] The aggregation is determined by the R&D intensities of industries (see Table 16). Section IV provides a detailed description of the database and the division of the manufacturing sector into the two industries.
[43] In 1990, Stora acquired Feldmühle and SCA acquired Reedpack.

Figure 24. Accumulated total foreign direct investment (FDI) in Schumpeter-industries and Heckscher-Ohlin-industries, 1982-92: deflated by the GDP implicit price index (1984 = 100), annual data.

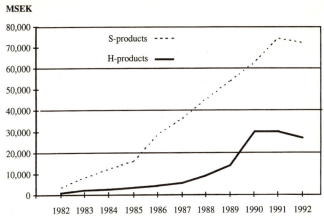

Note: Schumpeter (S) denotes knowledge-intensive industries and Heckscher-Ohlin (H) refers to basic industries.

Sources: Based on data from the Swedish central bank (FDI) and Statistics Sweden (implicit price index).

The huge increase in FDI in Heckscher-Ohlin industries in 1990 was followed by a correspondingly dramatic fall in 1991 and 1992. Altogether, there was a foreign divestment in Heckscher-Ohlin industries of about SEK 4 billion in current prices in 1991 and 1992, while Schumpeter industries invested approximately SEK 16 billion abroad. In 1987 and 1988 the level of investment in Schumpeter industries was almost twice the investment in Heckscher-Ohlin industries. As is seen from Figure 24, the overall picture seems to suggest that the Heckscher-Ohlin industries experienced a tendency towards increase in FDI after 1987, whereas the FDI in the Schumpeter industries shifted up earlier and remained at a constantly higher level.

To summarize the evolution during the 1980s, foreign investment has shifted markedly towards the Union and this trend has been particularly strong in the more knowledge-intensive industries.

II. The Theoretical Rationale for Outsider
Firms to locate within the European Union

International integration theory is normally confined to the partial effects of trade creation and trade diversion, where the former carries positive welfare implications in contrast to the negative effects associated with trade diversion. Recent contributions along this line of research, still in a partial framework, take into account the effects of trade suppression, trade cost reductions and game theoretic aspects. A distinct characteristic of these models is, however, the negligence of factor flows between regions as a response to changing institutional settings. Despite rather extensive empirical evidence of the impact of institutional change on factor flows, few attempts have been made to incorporate this into economic modeling (Dunning 1989; Braunerhjelm 1994). The "new" growth theory does incorporate some of these aspects (Romer 1986), and the concepts of "investment creation" and "investment diversion" have been introduced recently (Sweeney 1993).

One reason for the arbitrary treatment of firms in an integration context, besides analytical and mathematical complexities, is the strong tradition of fixed factors in mainstream trade economics. More precisely, factors of production are assumed to be perfectly mobile between sectors within an economy, whereas they are treated as perfectly immobile between countries. This is quite inconsistent considering the dominant role of relatively footloose multinational firms in trade, international investments, and in the diffusion of technological knowledge and know-how (Dunning 1993).The inconsistency becomes even more obvious when the factor financial capital is emphasized.

The theory of the firm claims that internationalization, either by setting up subsidiaries or by relying on exports, occurs in order to protect a firm's proprietary assets from imitation and opportunistic behavior (Hymer 1960; Caves 1971; Buckley and Casson 1976, 1992; Williamson 1975, 1985). Due to market failures, firms cannot engage in arm's-length contracts etc., without eroding their sources of competitiveness. Resourceseeking, tariff-jumping, global strategies etc. have also been suggested as reasons for internationalization (Mundell 1957; Hirsch 1976; Grant 1991). Price differences between markets are particularly important in vertical integration models, but the overwhelming argument for internationalization rests on the firms' possibility to exploit their firm-specific assets or knowledge, which is coherent with profit-maximizing behavior.

The driving forces behind firms' internationalization have been summarized in the eclectic approach by Dunning (1977) into three main factors: ownership advantages, location advantages (between countries) and the internalization of firms' proprietary assets. The EC 1992 program is expected to primarily affect the locational advantage by reducing production costs, improving the supportive systems for industries, and guaranteeing market access – thereby creating incentives for foreign firms to invest within the Union.

A shift in locational advantage, however, influences firms in different ways. Some firms base their competitiveness on the access to some country-specific, relatively abundant and inexpensive, natural resource or knowledge. Other firms derive their competitive edge from firm-specific factors, created within the firm through R&D and other knowledge-enhancing activities. A conspicuous feature of such firms is the participation in markets characterized by intensive technological competition where competitiveness requires continuous upgrading of know-how and skill (Eliasson 1991).

III. Hypotheses concerning Outsiders' Reactions to the EC 1992 Program

Keeping in perspective the evolution of Swedish FDI demonstrated above and the theoretical discussion, two hypotheses are formulated and exposed to empirical tests. First, if conditions for industrial production change between regions, firms in the Schumpeter industries are expected to be more apt to relocate, than firms in the Heckscher-Ohlin industries. One reason is that the Schumpeter industries can more easily take up production abroad, since their competitiveness does not depend on country-specific advantages (such as natural resources). Furthermore, since economies of scale are derived on the firm level in the Schumpeter industry, multi-plant production in several countries is facilitated. Heckscher-Ohlin firms, on the other hand, are characterized by huge investments in process-intensive plants undertaken at relatively long intervals (15-20 years) and at comparatively high costs. In downstream production, however, where operations are less capital-intensive, continuous foreign invest-

Figure 25. Swedish domestic gross investment (DGI) and foreign direct invest-ment (FDI) in the European Community, in Schumpeter- and Heckscher-Oh-lin-industries, 1982-92: deflated by the GDP implicit price index (1984=100).

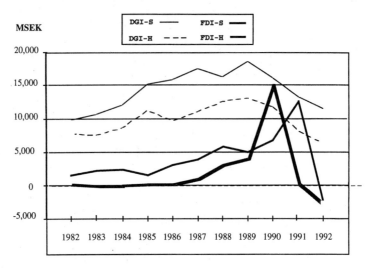

Note: Schumpeter (S) denotes knowledge-intensive industries and Heckscher-Ohlin (H) refers to basic industries.

Sources: Based on data from the Swedish central bank (FDI) and Statistics Sweden (implicit price index).

ments may occur in sales offices, service departments and other comple-mentary activities. Overall, this means comparatively higher locational flexibility in Schumpeter industries.[44]

The second hypothesis concerns the relation between foreign and domestic investment. Foreign direct investments are expected to a nega-tively impact home country investments. Although evidence is scattered, contemporary research also seems to indicate that large FDI has a crowd-ing out effect on domestic investment (Belderbos 1992; Lipsey and Ste-vens 1992). From a financial point of view such a relationship has often been claimed to exist, since home country investments compete with for-eign direct investments for scarce funds in terms of firms' retained earn-ings. However, although budget restrictions exist, we may argue that, in a world characterized by close to perfect financial integration, the financial

[44] These basic differences across industries became apparent in an extensive question-naire and interview study covering approximately 40% of the employees in the Swedish manufacturing sector (Braunerhjelm 1990).

argument should be of minor importance. In the case of Sweden, evidence exists that the Swedish financial markets were already *de facto* integrated when the EC 1992 program was first presented (Oxelheim 1990). Hence, the substitutional relationship we expect to find should be generated on the production side of the firm and be particularly apparent when firms are exposed to exogenous institutional shocks, as was the case with the EC 1992 program.

As shown in Figure 25, there seem to be apparent differences concerning the relationship between FDI and domestic gross investment (DGI) within the two industries. In Heckscher-Ohlin industries the flow figures indicate that investment abroad and at home follow a parallel pattern. They increased between 1982 and 1989, peaked between 1989 and 1990, and then fell significantly in 1991, indicating a complementary relationship. Schumpeter industries display a different pattern. Except for the years 1986 and 1990, the investment patterns seem to move in different directions. Noteworthy also is that in 1991 FDI in Schumpeter industries almost leveled for the first time with DGI, exceeding by far the total – foreign and domestic – investments undertaken in the Heckscher-Ohlin industries.

IV Data, Model and Empirical Results

As mentioned above, the Swedish manufacturing sector has been classified into two sectors, where the R&D intensities of industries determine whether they are classified as Schumpeterian or Heckscher-Ohlinian (Table 16). More precisely, the Schumpeter industry consists of ISIC 35 (chemicals) and 38 (engineering), while the Heckscher-Ohlin industry comprises ISIC 32 (textiles), 33 (wood), 34 (paper and pulp), and 37 (metal processing). Further specification in the composition of these aggregates is hindered by the lack of data. The two sub-industries ISIC 31 (food and beverage) and ISIC 36 (non-metallic mineral products) are excluded, since these industries have a history of heavy protection.

It can always be argued that the division undertaken here is artificial, since the operations of most firms involve both Schumpeterian and Heckscher-Ohlinian features. Attention will therefore be paid to the robustness of the results due to the different ways of treating borderline cases such as paper and pulp firms with fairly large high-tech content and chemistry firms involving production of both basic chemicals and pharmaceuticals.

Table 16. Research and development expenses in Swedish multinationals, 1986 and 1990: R&D expenses as percentage of turnover.

Industries	1986	1990
Food and beverage	0.7	0.2
Textiles	0.1	1.0
Paper & pulp	0.7	1.3
Chemicals	6.7	8.1
Metal processing	0.2	0.8
Engineering	4.5	5.3

Note: The figures are based on the IUI database covering Swedish multinationals. R&D expenses in industries not mentioned in the table are negligible. Unfortunately no data are available for the wood and non-metallic mineral products. However, these are known to have low R&D intensity.

Table 17. Correlation between annual changes in FDI and DGI, 1982-1991.

Type of investment	DGI-H	DGI-S
FDI-Heckscher-Ohlin (TOTAL)	-0.03 (0.94)	–
FDI-Schumpeter (TOTAL)	–	-0.23 (0.56)
FDI-Heckscher-Ohlin (EC)	0.26 (0.51)	–
FDI-Schumpeter (EC	–	-0.70 (0.03)

Note: Prob > | r | under Ho: $\zeta = 0$ are given in parentheses.

Correlation analyses reveal a significantly negative relationship in the period 1982-1991 between domestic investment and investment in the Union for Schumpeter industries, while no such relation can be found for Heckscher-Ohlin industries (Table 17). To be able to say anything more about this relationship, we have to resort to regression analyses.

Table 18. The relationship between foreign and domestic direct investment by firms in Schumpeter industries, 1982-1992.

Explanatory variables	Dependent variable = percentage change of foreign direct investment by knowledge-intensive Swedish industries into the European Community			
	Model 1	Model 2	Model 3	Model 4
Intercept	71.98 *** (4.24)	75.43 *** (4.54)	73.42 ** (3.65)	75.92 ** (3.82)
INVS$_d$	-2.27 ** (-2.51)	-2.26 ** (-2.59)	-2.46 (-1.66)	-2.33 (-1.60)
DUM92[a]	-224.58 *** (-4.83)	-220.63 *** (-4.90)	-224.56 *** (-4.48)	-220.64 *** (-4.47)
REXCH		-3.15 (-1.23)		-3.13 (-1.12)
CAP			1.49 (.17)	.53 (.06)
Adj R^2	.70	.73	.66	.67
F-value	11.67	8.86	6.71	5.54
DW	2.11	2.65	2.13	2.64

[a] In 1992, Swedish Schumpeter firms divested in the European Community.

Note: ***P<0.01; **P<0.05; *P<0.10.

The general form of the estimated equations is the following (all variables are expressed as percentage change):

$$INVS_{ec} = a_1 + a_2 INVS_d + a_3 REXCH + a_4 CAP + a_5 DUM92 + u$$
$$INVHO_{ec} = a_1 + a_2 INVHO_d + a_3 REXCH + a_4 CAP + a_5 DUM92 + u,$$

where INVSec and INVHOec denote investment within the Union by the knowledge-intensive (Schumpeter) industry and the Heckscher-Ohlin industry, respectively. INVSd and INVHOd are domestic investment by the two industries, respectively. REXCH and CAP represent the control variables: real exchange rates and capacity utilization. The REXCH variable is aimed at capturing swings in FDI due to the role of this variable as an investment incentive (lower labor costs abroad) or as a factor influencing the timing of the FDI (low cost of acquisition). The inclusion also helps to mitigate the accounting effects of such swings when FDI flows are reported in domestic currency. A dummy variable, DUM92, is inserted to

Table 19. The relationship between foreign and domestic direct investment by firms in Heckscher-Ohlin industries, 1982-92.

Explanatory variables	Dependent variable = percentage change of foreign direct investment by by the Heckscher-Ohlin part of Swedish industries into the European Community			
	Model 1	Model 2	Model 3	Model 4
Intercept	60.33 (1.16)	56.95 (1.03)	42.08 (0.85)	41.98 (0.77)
INVHO$_d$	2.10 (0.84)	1.82 (0.67)	6.59 (1.72)	6.42 (1.41)
DUM92[a]	-1,062.50 *** (-6.41)	-1,078.55 *** (-6.10)	-1056.50 *** (-6.90)	-1059.39 *** (-6.21)
REXCH		5.60 (.55)		.95 (.09)
CAP			-42.50 (-1.49)	-41.37 (-1.23)
Adj R^2	0.87	0.85	0.89	0.86
F	30.76	18.57	24.70	15.47
DW	1.98	2.35	2.88	2.89

[a] In 1992, Swedish Heckscher-Ohlin firms divested in the EC.

Note: See Table 18.

capture the effect after 1991 of the dramatic downturn in the business cycle, together with the fact that Sweden submitted its application for a Union membership in mid 1991. The period stretches between 1982 and 1992. Standard properties of the error term (uncorrelated and normally distributed) are assumed.

The data on FDI – of which some are unpublished – have been provided by the Swedish central bank, while data on DGI (output deflators and capacity utilization) were submitted by Statistics Sweden (SCB). Exchange rates are from the IMF database on international financial statistics and are based on relative, normalized unit labor costs.

Based on the discussion in previous sections, and the correlation results, we expect a negative relationship between foreign direct investment within the Union ($INVS_{ec}$) and domestic investment ($INVS_d$). The international recession, which has been particularly severe in Sweden, together with Sweden's application for membership to the Union in 1991, is expected to have a negative impact on investment abroad, which should be reflected in a negative value on the dummy variable. Changes in the control variables, the real exchange rate and capacity utilization are expected to exhibit a positive relationship with changes in foreign direct investment. Due to the scarcity of observations, we proceed stepwise. Hence, we will first discuss a test for each of these variables separately, followed by a test where all control variables are included.

If the negative relationship still exists between domestic and foreign direct investment after controlling for costs and capacity variables, the relationship has to be attributed to factors not captured in the regression analysis. Among those factors, institutional changes are assumed to be of major importance, that is, the EC 1992 program launched in 1985/1986 provides a natural explanation for the shift in investment towards the Union by Swedish firms. The results are summarized in Tables 18 and 19. All variables are expressed as a percentage of change.

The overall fit for Schumpeter industries is highly satisfactory considering the limited amount of observations, as are the F-values and the Durbin-Watson statistics. Domestic investment exhibits a significantly negative relationship with foreign direct investment in the first and second model. As capacity utilization is included in the estimations, however, this relationship loses its significance. To a large extent, this is a combined effect of the low number of degrees of freedom and a high multi-collinearity between changes in domestic investment and capacity utilization. On the other hand, neither capacity utilization nor the real exchange rates lend any statistical support in explaining foreign investment by Swedish firms. This also holds true when the regression excludes changes in domestic investment and is run with only the control variables as explanatory variables. The dummy variable supports the hypothesis that firms changed their behavior in 1992, faced by the slump in demand and the fact that Sweden applied for full membership in the Union.

Table 19 shows a positive relationship between investment at home and in the Union for firms in Heckscher-Ohlin industries, as is the case for the real exchange rate variable. However, in both cases the coefficients are insignificant.

The empirical results suggest that in the 1980s Swedish firms in the knowledge-intensive industries, confronted by the institutional change emanating from the EC 1992 program and the uncertainty concerning the future association between Sweden and the Union, substituted domestic for foreign investment.

V. Conclusions

We have found that a substantial shift in the investment pattern occurred at the time of the announcement of the EC 1992 program. The shift implied a dramatic increase in Swedish FDI in the Union, especially within Schumpeter industries. An interview study indicated that a major cause for this shift was uncertainty about a future Swedish Union membership and a fear of Fortress Europe, although other factors such as uncertainty about environmental and energy policies, high domestic production costs, etc., also had an impact (Braunerhjelm 1990).

As far as production is concerned, many studies have reported a positive effect of foreign production on the export of firms (Blomström, Lipsey and Kulchycky 1988; Kravis and Lipsey 1988; Swedenborg 1979). Some of these studies also included a positive relationship with regard to Swedish home country export and foreign production, although this result recently has been challenged in an approach that also includes exports from Swedish subsidiaries (Svensson 1993). In this chapter we stretch the relationship somewhat further and emphasize the relationship between domestic and foreign direct investment. In doing so, we have found no sign of complementarity.

On the contrary, we have found strong substitutability between investment abroad and at home in the Schumpeter industry. However, these findings are only significant for the Union region, that is, the core economic area for Swedish multinational firms, whereas the pattern is less pronounced when the whole world is considered. We were unable to explain the shift of investment by invoking factors related to the Swedish economy. Instead the results support an influence from other factors, particularly the institutional change represented by the EC 1992 program, as a major determinant of the inflows of Swedish investment to the Union. The results are robust as regards the aggregation. If the borderline case – ISIC 34 – had been moved into the category of Schumpeter industries, the findings would have been made even stronger.

In the long run, a diminished Schumpeter industry could have severe welfare consequences. If increasingly larger proportions of the R&D-intensive sector are located abroad, higher macroeconomic vulnerability would be introduced into the Swedish economy due to greater dependence on more price-sensitive, basic production. Further, an erosion of knowledge or skill today may be extremely hard to recapture later, especially if the future location of firms is governed by already existing clusters, for example, to take advantage of R&D spillovers. Hence, a shift today may have irreversible long-term effects on the production structure and the welfare level in outsider countries. Such changes in the core of Swedish manufacturing industries – the top-ten value added contributors – have been reported by Oxelheim and Gärtner (1994), and are discussed in the next chapter.

Considering the size of the shift in investment and the substitutability found for knowledge-intensive industries, policy makers in outsider countries have to take into account the macroeconomic effects originating from the footlooseness of firms excluded from institutional arrangements such as the EC 92 program, LAFTA, NAFTA, etc. Such effects should not be neglected since structural imbalances in the domestic industry could, as emphasized in the "new" growth theory, trap countries in different, long-term growth paths (Baldwin 1989).

References

Andersson, T. and T. Fredriksson (1993): *Sveriges val, EG och direktinvesteringar.* Report for the Ministry of Finance. Bilaga 7 till EG-konsekvensutredningen, Samhällsekonomi. Stockholm: Allmänna förlaget.

Baldwin, R. (1989): The Growth Effects of 1992. *Economic Policy 4*: 249-281.

Belderbos, R. (1992): Large Multinational Enterprises Based in a Small Economy: Effect on Domestic Investments. *Weltwirtschaftliches Archiv 128*: 543-558.

Blomström, M., R. E. Lipsey and K. Kulchycky (1988): US and Swedish Direct Investment and Exports. In R. Baldwin (ed.) *Trade Policy Issues and Empirical Analysis.* Chicago: University of Chicago Press.

Braunerhjelm, P. (1990): *Svenska industriföretag inför EG 1992.* Stockholm: IUI.

Braunerhjelm, P. (1994): *Regional Integration and the Location of Knowledge-Intensive Multi-National Firms: Implications for Comparative Advantage and Welfare of Outsiders and Insiders.* Dissertation. Stockholm: *Working Paper*, No. 404, IUI.

Buckley, P. and M. Casson (1976): *The Future of the Multinational Enterprise.* London: Macmillan.

Buckley, P. and M. Casson (1992): Organizing for Innovation: The Multinational Enterprise in the Twenty-first Century, in P. Buckley and M. Casson (ed.) *Multinational Enterprises in the World Economy.* Aldershot: Edward Elgar Publishing Ltd.

Buigues, P. and A. Jacquemin (1989): Strategies of Firms and Structural Environments in the Large Internal Market. *Journal of Common Market Studies 28*: 53-67.

Burgenmeier, B. and J. L. Mucchielli (ed.) (1991): *Multinationals and Europe 1992.* London: Routledge.

Caves, R. (1971): International Corporations: The Industrial Economics of Foreign Investment. *Economica 38*: 1-27.

Dunning, J. (1977): Trade, Location of Economic Activity and the MNE: A Search for an Eclectic Approach, in B. Ohlin, P.-O. Hesselborn and P.-M. Wijkman, (ed.) *The International Allocation of Economic Activity: Proceedings of a Nobel Symposium at Stockholm.* London: Macmillan.

Dunning, J. (1989): European Integration and Transatlantic Foreign Direct Investment: The Record Assessed, in G.N. Yannopoulous (ed.)

Europe and America, 1992: US-EC Economic Relations and the Single European Market. Manchester: Manchester University Press.

Dunning, J. (1993): International Direct Investment Patterns in the 1990s. In Oxelheim, L. (ed.) *The Global Race for Foreign Direct Investment: Prospects for the Future*. Berlin: Springer Verlag.

Eliasson, G. (1991): The Firm as a Competitive Team. *Journal of Economic Behavior and Organization 13*: 273-289.

Grant, R. (1991): *Contemporary Strategic Analysis*. Oxford: Basil Blackwell.

Hirsch, S. (1976): An International Trade and Investment Theory of the Firm. *Oxford Economic Papers 28*: 258-269.

Hirsch, S. and A. Meshulach (1992): *Towards a Unified Theory of Internationalization*. Business and Economic Studies on European Integration, Working Paper 1/92. Copenhagen: Copenhagen Business School.

Hymer, S. (1960): *The International Operations of National Firms: A Study of Direct Foreign Investment*. Dissertation. Cambridge: MIT Press.

Karlsen, J. (1990): *Business Strategy and National Policy Concerning Integration: Nordic Direct Foreign Investments in the European Community*. Notat 25/90. Bergen: NØI.

Kravis, I. and R. E. Lipsey (1988): The Effects of Multinational Firms' Foreign Operations on their Domestic Employment. *Working Paper*, No. 2760. New York: National Bureau of Economic Research.

Lipsey, R. and G. Stevens (1992): Interactions Between Domestic and Foreign Investment. *Journal of International Money and Finance 11*: 40-62.

Mundell, R. (1957): International Trade and Factor Mobility. *American Economic Review. 47*: 321-335.

Oxelheim, L. (1990): *International Financial Integration*. Berlin: Springer-Verlag.

Oxelheim, L. (1993): Foreign Direct Investment and the Liberalization of Capital Movements. In Oxelheim, L. (ed.) *The Global Race for Foreign Direct Investment: Prospects for the Future*. Berlin: Springer-Verlag.

Oxelheim, L. and R. Gärtner (1994): Small Country Manufacturing Industries in Transition – the Case of the Nordic Region. *Management International Review 4*, Vol 34, 1994/4, pp. 331-356.

Ozawa, T. (1992): Cross-investment between Japan and the EC: Income Similarity, Product Variation, and Economies of Scope. In Cantwell, J. (ed.) *Multinational Investment in Modern Europe: Strategic Interaction in the Integrated Community*. Aldershot: Edward Elgar Publishing.

Romer, P. (1986): Increasing Returns and Long-Run Growth. *Journal of Political Economy 94*: 1002-1037.

Rugman, A. and S. Verbeke (1991): Competitive Strategies for Non-European Firms. In B. Burgenmeier and Mucchielli (ed.) *Multinationals and Europe 1992*. London: Routledge.

Svensson, R. (1993): *Production in Foreign Affairs – Effects on Home Country Exports and Modes of Entry*. Thesis. Göteborg: Göteborg University.

Swedenborg, B. (1979): *The Multinational Operations of Swedish Firms: An Analysis of Determinants and Effects*. Stockholm: IUI.

Sweeney, R. (1993): The International Competition for Foreign Direct Investment. In Oxelheim, L. (ed.) *The Global Race for Foreign Direct Investment: Prospects for the Future*. Berlin: Springer-Verlag.

US International Trade Commission (1992): *The Effects of Greater Economic Integration within the European Community on the United States: Fourth Following Report*. Washington, DC: US International Trade Commission.

Venables, A. (1994): Economic Integration and Industrial Agglomeration, *The Economic and Social Review*, Vol. 26, pp. 1-17.

Williamson, O. (1975): *Market and Hierarchies: Analysis and Antitrust Implications*. New York: Free Press.

Williamson, O. (1985): *The Economic Institutions of Capitalism*. New York: Free Press.

Yamawaki, H. (1990): *Locational Decisions of Japanese Multinational Firms in European Manufacturing Industries*. Berlin: Science Center, mimeo.

Yannopoulous, G. (1990): Foreign Direct Investment and European Integration: Evidence from the Formative Years of the European Community. *Journal of Common Market Studies 28*: 235-259.

Yannopoulous, G. (1992): Multinational Corporations and the Single European Market. In Cartwell, J. (ed.), *Multinational Investment in Modern Europe: Strategic Interaction in the Integrated Community*. Aldershot: Edward Elgar Publishing.

Chapter 5:
Home Country Effects
from Outward FDI

A Regional Study of Changes in
Production Patterns[45]

Lars Oxelheim and Robert Gärtner

In the previous chapters, we have seen some empirical evidence for a change in the investment behavior of industries in small countries outside the European Union. According to the hypotheses put forward in Chapter 2 (see, for instance, the exemplified decision matrix of companies located in non-Union countries), industries in small outsiders should react to the perceived threat of a Fortress Europe by out-locating production to the Union. By measuring flows of foreign direct investment (FDI) from a number of small outsiders (Austria, Finland, Israel, Norway and Sweden) into the Union and the United States, the hypothesized behavior was substantiated. Under the assumption that the response to the formation of an internal market should primarily affect the knowledge-intensive parts of the industry, Chapter 4 continued the analysis by dividing the flows of Swedish FDI by knowledge intensity and host country. The analysis provided empirical support that a substitutory relationship existed for 1982-1992 between direct investment in the Union and direct investment at home by knowledge-intensive Swedish companies.

In this chapter, we hypothesize that a response similar to the one presented by Braunerhjelm and Oxelheim in Chapter 4 should apply to other predominantly small outsider countries with close trade relationships to the Union. However, due to lack of data, the same methodology is not applicable to other small outsiders. Thus, in order to examine whether the result of the Swedish analysis also holds true for other small outsiders, we have to adopt an alternative approach. Hence, we will herein capture the effects of a substitutory relationship by focusing on home country effects.

---

[45] This chapter is in part based on findings reported in Oxelheim and Gärtner (1994).

We will study changes in production patterns as expressed by changes in the value added of the core manufacturing industry. We expect the substitutory relationship for the period 1982-1992 to express itself in a decline in the knowledge intensity of the core of domestic manufacturing industries of outsider countries.

Due to the homogeneity of the Nordic region, the choice of the Nordic countries[46] as study objects offers opportunities to make comparisons and to analyze the home country effect of regionalization in general, and of the Union in particular, on the production pattern of a small open economy. Being located in small outsider countries, the Finnish and Norwegian manufacturing industries should exhibit the same behavior as the core of the corresponding Swedish manufacturing industries and out-locate (primarily) knowledge-intensive production to the Union. Moreover, the decrease in knowledge intensity in the manufacturing industries, which is expected to take place in these countries, should have no correspondence in the insider country, Denmark. Rather, in a longer perspective, an upgrading should be the case.

Throughout history, the cultural and linguistic similarities of the Nordic countries have resulted in a number of attempts at intra-Nordic agreements and resolutions of economic cooperation across borders. Looking back in history, the intra-Nordic borders have changed or been erased, making the Nordic area sometimes consist of fewer than the current five countries. In terms of similarities, from the end of the Second World War until the end of the 1980s, the Nordic countries were all characterized by the extensive use of capital controls. As shown by Oxelheim (1995), these controls became *de facto* inefficient prior to the *de jure* dismantling, which occurred in Denmark in 1988, in Sweden in 1989, in Norway in 1990, and finally in Finland in 1991. All the Nordic economies may be labeled public economies, since the total tax burden is very high. In 1992, the Swedish and Danish tax burdens were the highest in the world, with Norway sharing fourth place with the Netherlands.

Institutional differences among the Nordic countries do exist. From a policy point of view, Danish policy-making has been market oriented, while politicians in the other Nordic countries have demonstrated a high propensity to regulate (Oxelheim 1995). Moreover, Denmark is a member of the Union, whereas Finland, Norway and Sweden were candidates for membership, and Finland and Sweden are now members.

---

[46] Iceland is excluded from this study.

At an aggregated level, all the three outsider countries reveal signs of having been through a period of industrial restructuring. As mentioned in Chapter 2, Finland, Norway and Sweden have all experienced dramatic outflows of direct investment during the latter half of the 1980s. In terms of net flows of FDI as a percentage of GDP for 1986-1990, among OECD countries Sweden shows the highest gap between outward and inward investment (3.44% outward and 0.56% inward). Finland also exhibits a large gap (1.96% outward and 0.46% inward), whereas Norway (1.44% and 0.90%), and Denmark (1.04% and 0.54%) show a small average net outflow of half a percentage point (OECD 1992). Furthermore, in contrast to Denmark, all three outsiders have experienced a decrease in the manufacturing sector as a percentage of GDP. Hence, between 1976 and 1992, the Finnish manufacturing sector shrunk 7.9 percentage points to 18.8%, the Norwegian sector declined 6.1 percentage points to 13.4% and the Swedish sector decreased 7.0 percentage points to 17.6%, while the Danish manufacturing sector increased 1.6 percentage points to 16.5% of the total Danish GDP. However, although the manufacturing sector in all the Nordic countries is small, the major part of exports comes from this sector, indicating that the stakes may be high in the light of a possible Fortress Europe.

Since data on foreign direct investment by Danish, Norwegian and Finnish companies comparable to those used by Braunerhjelm and Oxelheim in Chapter 4 are not obtainable (and not even registered), in this chapter we study home country effects ensuing from outward FDI by using corporate data. Based on the well-supported assumption that most FDI in manufacturing industries is undertaken by the largest companies, we will focus on the ten largest companies of each country. These largest companies are also chosen as the object of study, since they constitute the core of the national production network and account for much of the spillover in know-how and managerial skills, which is the sound base for future national prosperity. Furthermore, by focusing on large manufacturing companies, we hope to capture the major aggregated effects on the industrial sector since large companies also account for a large proportion of total output and employment.

In addition, we analyze other structural changes in the top-ten group that may have been brought about by foreign direct investment activity such as the degree of internationalization, concentration in terms of industry classification, as well as of the relative contribution to the entire manufacturing part of GDP.

I. Definitions and Data Problems

The focus of this study is on the largest Nordic manufacturing companies. To be classified as a manufacturing company, more than 50% of the company's revenue has to originate from manufacturing activities. Another criterion is that the company has to be listed on the local stock market. Iceland is excluded from this study because her stock market has only recently emerged. Hence, this study encompasses Denmark, Finland, Norway and Sweden. The stock market criterion and its consequences for the outlook of national companies are further discussed in a later section. Each company is classified on a two-digit basis according to its main economic activity (in terms of revenues) in line with ISIC (International Standard Industrial Classification of all Economic Activities).

We use the distribution of value added as a major indicator of changes in production patterns. Value added has the attractive characteristic of overriding sectoral distortions with respect to use of capital, labor or raw-material intensive processes of production. As compared with sales, for instance, it better reflects the importance of the sectors for the economy. Value added is defined as the sum of the operating result (before depreciation), wages, salaries, social costs and other remuneration paid to the employees and to the board of the company. The ten largest companies of each Nordic country are ranked according to total value added. In order to reflect the importance of the top-ten companies relative to domestic value added in manufacturing, total value added is split into a foreign and a domestic part. The relative number of employees in the country of the parent company serves as weighting in this split.[47] Calculations are based on data from annual reports and interviews. The Nordic accounting practice is fairly harmonized and annual reports from different Nordic countries are compatible with each other and with the General Agreed Accounting Principles (GAAP).

In separating value added from knowledge-intensive companies from value added generated in other companies, R&D intensity is used as indicator. As reported in Braunerhjelm and Oxelheim (1992), in 1990 the R&D expenses as a percentage of the turnover of Swedish multinational

---

[47] Whereas Swedish corporate annual reports provide sufficient information for a correct division of value added into a part generated at home as well as abroad, Finnish, Danish and Norwegian corporate statements do not. When comparing Swedish companies' actual domestic and foreign value added with domestic and foreign value added arrived at using relative employment as weight, the fit is close to perfect. Assuming the proxy fits well also for the other countries in the study, the estimate should be adequate to illustrate the importance of the top-ten groups for local GDP.

companies were 8.1 and 5.3 for ISIC 35 (chemicals) and 38 (engineering) respectively, whereas for other ISIC groups they were considerably smaller; around or below 1%. For Finnish manufacturing companies in ISIC 38, the 1989 R&D expenses as a percentage of turnover averaged 3%. For companies of ISIC 33 and 34 (wood, paper and pulp), the average was below 1%. We here assume that a similar pattern exists also in the other Nordic countries and classify companies belonging to ISIC 35 and 38 as knowledge intensive. Large companies are, however, typically multi-product and multi-plant in character, which creates classification problems (see Eliasson, Fölster, Lindberg, Pousette and Taymaz 1990, Hirsch and Thomsen 1993). Thus, aggregated figures for knowledge intensity may include some "noise" in terms of small contributions from other ISIC groups. Hence, the figures have to be interpreted as indicative only.

The analysis covers primarily the period 1982-1992,[48] the starting and ending years of which are similar in major respects: general economic problems and exchange rate turbulence characterize both years in all the Nordic countries under study here. The use of 1982 as a year of comparison is motivated by our ambition to control for effects generated by changes in the real exchange rate. Such changes may provide investment incentives as well as influence the timing of the investment, leading to large swings in the value of FDI stocks when reported in local currency. Thus, our choice of period represents a possible way to avoid the necessity of correcting for such accounting effects.

II. The largest Nordic Manufacturing Companies – Distributions of Size and Activity

Appendix I illustrates the relative sizes among the top-ten companies in 1992 within as well as between the countries. As in 1982, Swedish companies in 1992 were giants as compared with their Danish, Norwegian and Finnish counterparts. According to sales, in 1982 Volvo was by far the largest Swedish company. In 1992, it kept that position, but (as can be seen by the moderate discrepancy between the average and median sales figures) Volvo is no longer enjoying splendid isolation: Electrolux and the other Swedish companies are not trailing far behind. On the other hand,

---

[48] The figures of the year of comparison - 1982 - are based on findings reported in Oxelheim (1984).

in 1992 as in 1982, Norway harbored one outlier among the top-ten group of companies: Norsk Hydro. Neither in Denmark nor in Finland can such an outlier be found among the top-ten companies.

The ten largest manufacturing companies are ranked and listed by total value added in 1992 in Appendices II to V. Figures for 1982 are also provided in the appendices. For various reasons, to be discussed at a later stage in this chapter, some companies represented in the 1992 top-ten groups did not qualify for the 1982 top-ten groups. In 1992, total value added figures for the top-ten groups in Denmark, Finland, Norway and Sweden – expressed as a percentage of value added for domestic manufacturing industries – were 19, 50, 53 and 57, respectively. In a Nordic context, the total nominal value added of the top ten Swedish manufacturing companies stands out as being very large; about 6% larger than the entire Danish manufacturing sector, 64% larger than the entire Norwegian manufacturing sector, and 20% larger than the entire Finnish manufacturing sector. Value added in domestic operations of the ten largest companies accounted for 11%, 28%, 30% and 23% of manufacturing value added in Denmark, Finland, Norway and Sweden respectively.

Danish Manufacturing Companies

As compared with 1982, total value added in 1992 from the ten largest Danish manufacturing companies relative to the entire manufacturing part of Danish GDP was up one percentage point. Judging from the value added figures of the top-five groups of 1982 and 1992, the increase can be attributed to the top-five companies.

In 1992, the domestic part of value added from the Danish top-ten manufacturing companies had dropped three percentage points since 1982 (see column 6 in Appendix II). The drop can be attributed to the top-five group of companies and indicates a decreasing relative importance of the core manufacturing companies as contributors to the generation of domestic value added.

Together, the Danish top-ten manufacturing companies that offer products based on chemicals (ISIC 35) increased their contribution by 0.7 percentage points and accounted domestically for 3.6% of Danish manufacturing value added (Novo and Superfos). The second largest product group – food processing (ISIC 31) – contributed 3.2% (Danisco and Carlsberg), a decline from 5.3% in 1982, when this product group was in majority. Machinery, electronics and metal products (ISIC 38) accounted for 2.7% of domestic manufacturing value added, a decrease of 2.0 percentage points since 1982, and the three companies representing cement and building materials (ISIC 36) contributed 1.4%, an increase of 0.6 percentage points since 1982.

Finnish Manufacturing Companies

In 1982, the ratio between total value added of the top ten Finnish manufacturing companies and value added in domestic manufacturing industries was 27%. Ten years later, the ratio had increased to about 50%. The figures for the top-five groups of 1982 and 1992 were 18% and 31%, respectively, revealing that the top-five group was responsible for a large part of the increase.

In 1982, the top-ten group accounted for 23% of the domestic value added from manufacturing companies. By 1992 the top-ten group figure had grown to 28% and can, to some extent, be attributed to the five largest companies, which (ranked according to their domestic contribution) represented 16% and 19% in 1982 and 1992, respectively.

Five of the Finnish 1992 top-ten companies produced machinery, metal products and/or electronics (ISIC 38), as compared with only three in 1982. Among the newcomers in ISIC 38 is Nokia, which during the 1980s converted its wood production to electronics, machinery and rubber. Between 1982 and 1992, the number of top-ten companies producing wood products (ISIC 33 and 34) shrunk, as did their contribution to domestic total manufacturing value added.

Norwegian Manufacturing Companies

The ten largest Norwegian manufacturing companies ranked according to total value added are exhibited in Appendix IV. In 1992, total value added from the Norwegian top-ten companies relative to the entire Norwegian manufacturing industry was approximately 53%, an increase of 22 percentage points since 1982. The top-five companies exhibited a corresponding increase.

Between 1982 and 1992, the top-five companies accounted for the entire increase of seven percentage points in the contribution to the domestic part of Norwegian manufacturing GDP displayed by the top-ten group.

As in 1982, the biggest contributor in 1992 to domestic value added was found in the activity group consisting of companies producing pharmaceuticals, chemicals and petrochemicals (ISIC 35), namely Norsk Hydro. In this group, Hafslund Nycomed has entered the list since 1982. Kværner and Aker (second and third on the total value added list, and fourth and third on the domestic value added list) represented another important product group; machinery (ISIC 38). In 1992, this duo's contribution to domestic manufacturing value added was 8.1%, a substantial increase since 1982.

Swedish Manufacturing Companies

In 1992, total value added of the Swedish top-ten companies relative to manufacturing value added in Sweden was down almost three percentage points since 1982, connoting higher growth in manufacturing GDP than in the group of top-ten companies. Total value added generated by the top-five companies relative to manufacturing GDP decreased five percentage points over the period.

Expressed as a decline of nine percentage points in the top-ten companies' contribution to domestic value added, the relative importance of the Swedish core manufacturing companies clearly decreased between 1982 and 1992. The top-five companies accounted for almost the entire drop.

By 1992, all Swedish top-ten companies that produced machinery, electronics and metal products (ISIC 38) exhibited a large decline since 1982 in terms of contribution to domestic manufacturing value added. Electrolux, for instance, more than halved its contribution to domestic value added. In 1992 the second largest contributors were to be found in food processing (ISIC 31) as well as wood, pulp and paper (ISIC 33, 34) – industries that did not make the top-ten list in 1982.

III. Real Growth of Nordic Manufacturing Industries

Table 20 displays the real percentage growth in value added for the four groups of top-ten companies, as well as for the entire manufacturing industries and total GDP. Between 1982 and 1992, none of the four countries exhibited negative real growth in either total or manufacturing GDP. Denmark's high growth in manufacturing value added between 1982 and 1992 was almost exactly reflected by real growth in total GDP. In this

Table 20. Real percentage growth in value added for four Nordic countries, 1982-1992.

Country	In total value added of the top-ten group	In domestic value added of the top-ten group	In value added of the entire manufacturing industry	In total GDP
Denmark	64	18	55	54
Finland	113	42	23	58
Norway	58	22	6	12
Sweden	17	-15	23	42

Note: Denmark's, Finland's and Norway's real growth figures have been deflated using indices for wholesale prices. Sweden's real growth figures have been deflated with indices for producer prices within ISIC category 3. The Finnish 1982 top-ten group has been modified so as to include Valmet, Outokumpo and Rautaruukki, the Norwegian 1982 top-ten group to include Hafslund Nycomed, and the Swedish to include Procordia.

respect, Denmark differs from the other three Nordic countries. Although real growth in Finnish, Norwegian and Swedish manufacturing industries has been positive, the higher real growth in total GDP makes the manufacturing sector of these economies constitute a decreasing share.

When it comes to the top-ten groups of companies, we want to investigate how the core of the respective manufacturing industry has changed over the period. However, over time the core companies may: i) have undergone restructuring and completely altered their main activity (Nokia, for instance, developed from a pulp and paper-dominated company – ISIC 34 – in 1982 to a company with electronics – ISIC 38 – as its main activity in 1992); or ii) include one or more companies that were omitted from the corresponding 1982 group due to ineligibility according to the stock market listing criterion. Valmet, Outokumpu, Rautaruukki, Hafslund Nycomed[49] and Procordia are all examples of the second category. Thus, when calculating the real growth of the core manufacturing groups between 1982 and 1992, the 1982 top-ten lists for Finland, Norway and Sweden have been modified so as to include these companies. Based on the modified 1982 top-ten lists, the highest real growth in total value added was exhibited by the Finnish group. The Finnish as well as the Norwe-

---

[49] Hafslund Nycomed was not eligible in 1982, since the company is the result of a merger in 1986 between Hafslund and Nyegaard and Co. However, the combined 1982 value added figures for these two companies - at that time classified as ISIC 35 and 38 respectively - are included in the 1982 figures in Appendixes 1 and 4, Tables 20, 22 and 23.

gian top-ten groups exhibited real growth in domestic value added that was higher than real growth in the entire manufacturing sector, indicating the importance of these groups to the growth process of their respective economy. A higher degree of internationalization among these groups is revealed by the fact that real growth in total value added was higher than in domestic value added.

In Table 21, real growth in total as well as domestic value added is exhibited for the individual 1992 top-ten companies. No individual top-ten Danish company exhibited negative real growth in total value added between 1982-1992. In this respect, Novo, Royal Copenhagen and NKT (originally Nordiske Kabel and Traadfabrikker) exhibited the highest growth. Novo, a biochemical firm, is ranked first not only in total and domestic value added (see Appendix II), but also exhibited the highest real growth in both total and domestic value added. Not far behind are Royal Copenhagen and NKT. Four out of the ten companies displayed negative real growth in domestic value added. Among those, we find Danisco, whose relative number of domestic employees was halved between 1982 and 1992. Over that period, all Danish top-ten companies showed higher real growth abroad than at home, reflecting increased internationalization.

All Finnish 1992 top-ten companies exhibited positive real growth in total value added between 1982 and 1992, whereas in terms of domestic value added, three companies did not. Domestic value added generated by the ISIC 38 company Metra, for instance, shrunk in real terms by more than 50% over the period. All Finnish top-ten companies grew faster in total, as opposed to domestic value added, indicating increased internationalization. Among the Finnish top-ten companies, the wood, pulp and paper company Repola exhibited the highest real growth in total value added, as well as in domestic value added.

In terms of real growth in total value added, one company stands out from the rest of the Norwegian top-ten companies: Orkla, a food processing company and the biggest in Norway within branded consumer goods. The very high figure of 722% is explained by the fact that the company started from a low nominal level in 1982, and has been subject to major restructuring and expansion since 1982. Other companies with high real growth in total value added are Freia Marabou, Rieber and Sons, Aker, Dyno and Kværner. Between 1982 and 1992, two companies (Elkem and Hafslund Nycomed) shrunk in real terms in total value added. Those companies exhibited negative real growth in domestic value added as well.

Table 21. Real percentage growth in value added in the individual top-ten companies in 1992.

Denmark		
	Real growth in value added 1982-92 (%)	
Company	Total	in Denmark
Novo	238	207
Danisco	102	-1
Carlsberg	33	-10
FLS Industrier	10	-42
NKT	173	97
Superfos	11	-30
Jens Villadsen	67	60
Portland	38	27
Royal Cop.	195	184
B&O	93	101
Total for the top-ten group	74.5	24.5

Finland		
	Real growth in value added 1982-92 (%)	
Company	Total	in Finland
Repola	253	120
Nokia	71	70
Outokumpu	234	65
Kymmene	106	51
Kone	93	-13
Valmet	126	70
Enso-Gutzeit	42	30
Metra	58	-52
Metsä-Serla	33	-2
Rautaruukki	82	43
Total for the top-ten group	104.0	32.8

Norway		
	Real growth in value added 1982-92 (%)	
Company	Total	in Norway
Norsk Hydro	42	31
Kvaerner	139	3
Aker	206	160
Orkla	722	644
Hafslund	-33	-58
Dyno	165	-28
Freia Marab.	488	192
Elkem	-30	-31
Norske Skog	76	73
Rieber & Son	277	132
Total for the top-ten group	74.3	37.3

Sweden		
	Real growth in value added 1982-92 (%)	
Company	Total	in Sweden
Electrolux	36	-50
Ericsson	6	6
Volvo	-20	-31
Procordia	160	78
Stora	383	166
SKF	-3	-36
SCA	193	37
Saab-Scania	-1	-18
Sandvik	22	-46
Astra	274	67
Total for the top-ten group	39.1	-3.7

Dyno, a fast growing company according to total value added, exhibited negative real growth according to domestic value added. Also in the case of the Norwegian top-ten companies, a process of internationalization is evident.

On the two extremes in terms of real growth in total value added of Swedish companies, we find Volvo, with a strong negative growth that made it slide from the number one position in 1982 to a third place in 1992, and Stora, which did not make the list in 1982. Stora had the highest real growth in total value added, almost 400%, awarding it a place among the top-five. SCA is another company of ISIC 33 and 34 that, thanks to high real growth in total value added (almost 200%), entered the 1992 top-ten list. The pharmaceutical company Astra grew almost 300% in total value added over the same period and has also entered the top-ten list since 1982. Procordia, the former state-owned Statsföretag, experienced a real growth of over 160% since 1982. Procordia's two main activities are food processing (42% of turnover in 1992), and pharmaceuticals and biochemicals (38% of the 1992 turnover).

Five of the Swedish top-ten companies exhibited negative real growth in domestic value added. One company – Stora – displayed real growth of more than 100%, while the slowest real growth was exhibited by Electrolux, number one on the total top-ten list. No company showed real growth in domestic value added higher than real growth in total value added (which also goes for Ericsson when decimals are considered), a sign of an ongoing (if not accentuated) process of internationalization.

Development of employment

Changes in the real growth of the top ten groups may also be expressed in terms of changes in domestic employment. In Table 22, the number of domestic employees as a percentage of the total number of employees for the 1982 and the 1992 top-ten groups of companies is listed. As has been illustrated by our value added figures and also emphasized by, for instance, Heum and Ylä-Anttila (1992), all four top-ten groups exhibited a noticeable decrease in the share of domestic employees, describing the ongoing process of internationalization.

IV. The Knowledge Intensity of Nordic Industries

In Table 23, the top-ten companies of the Nordic countries are grouped by main activity and contribution to domestic value added. The table not only exhibits the distribution of activities but is the basis for a discussion about the hypothesis regarding knowledge-intensive industries, which was first addressed in the introduction of this chapter. According to that hypothesis, the domestic value added contribution of the Finnish, Norwegian and Swedish knowledge-intensive companies (ISIC 35 and 38) should have decreased over the period from 1982 to 1992; whereas, at least in the long run, the opposite should be true in the case of Denmark.

Table 22. Domestic employment as a percentage of the total number of employees for the 1982 and 1992 top-ten groups in four Nordic countries

Country	1982	1992	Decrease 1982-1992, percent
Denmark	81	58	28
Finland	85	57	33
Norway	72	56	23
Sweden	56	41	27

Note: The 1982 figures are based on the modified top-ten list as used in Table 1, i.e., Valmet, Outokumpu and Rautaruukki are included in the Finnish 1982 figures, Hafslund Nycomed in the Norwegian 1982 figures, and Procordia in the Swedish.

The knowledge-intensive groups are isolated in Table 23, thus revealing any change in the relative contribution of these groups to the total domestic manufacturing value added (knowledge contribution of the top-ten group), as well as to value added of the top-ten manufacturing companies of the four countries (knowledge intensity within the top-ten group). In a contrast to changes in knowledge intensity, knowledge contribution reflects changes in concentration.

As was noted in the previous section, changes over time in the core manufacturing industries may occur. Hence, in order to properly describe these changes in the pattern of knowledge contribution and knowledge intensity among the four countries, contributions from Valmet, Outokumpu, Rautaruukki, Hafslund Nycomed and Procordia have been included in the 1982 figures in Table 23.

The Danish top-ten group exhibited a somewhat scattered pattern in 1992, as it did in 1982, when equally many ISIC categories were represented. However, changes can be observed: ISIC 35 lost two companies to ISIC 36. The almost 2% lower knowledge contribution is explained by the fact that the contribution to manufacturing value added from ISIC 38 decreased since 1982. This contradicts our *a priori* view of an insider. However, the result reflects a decreased degree of concentration, which in fact hides a slight upward change in knowledge intensity within the top-ten group (from 57% in 1982 to 58% in 1992).

Although Valmet, Outokumpo (both ISIC 38) and Rautaruukki (ISIC 37) are included in the Finnish 1982 figures in Table 23, ISIC 33 and 34 dominated in 1982 as in 1992 in terms of contribution to domestic value added, but not in the number of companies. Activity concentration remained unchanged, while the relative contribution from all four ISIC

Table 23. The top-ten companies of 1992 and 1982 by activity groups and contribution to domestic value added in four Nordic countries.

Main activity (activity code - ISIC)	Number of companies 1992 and 1982 in							
	Denmark		Finland		Norway		Sweden	
	1992	1982	1992	1982	1992	1982	1992	1982
Food processing (31)	2(3.2)	2(5.3)			3(6.6)	1(2.1)	1(4.0)	1(2.8)
Textiles (32)								
Saw mills, pulp and paper (33,34)			4(15.2)	4(13.1)	1(2.0)	1(1.2)	2(4.1)	
Chemicals (35)	2(3.6)	4(3.5)			3(11.3)	4(13.0)	1(1.4)	
Goods from minerals (36)	3(1.4)	1(0.8)				1(1.9)		1(2.8)
Iron. steel. non ferrous metals (37)			1(2.3)	1(2.0)	1(1.6)	1(2.5)	1(1.2)	
Machinery, metal products. electronics (38)	3(2.7)	3(4.7)	5(10.7)	5(9.4)	2(8.1)	2(5.0)	5(12.5)	8(28.2)
Other manufacturing (39)								
Total relative contribution to the domestic manufacturing value added (%);	10.9	14.3	28.2	24.5	29.6	25.7	23.2	33.8
of which the knowledge-intensive part (ISIC35+38) represents (percentage points)	6.3	8.2	10.7	9.4	19.4	18.0	13.9	28.2

Note: The figures in the table are in some instances different from those found in the country tables (Appendices II to V). One difference is, as in the case with Tables 1 and 3, that the 1982 top ten groups have been altered so as to include companies that have been listed on the stock market between 1982 and 1992 and should have made a top-ten list in 1982. Concretely, this means that Valmet, Outokumpu and Rautaruukki have been included on the Finnish 1982 top-ten list, Hafslund Nycomed on the Norwegian 1982 top-ten list, and Procordia on the Swedish 1982 top-ten list. The Danish 1982 contribution figure differs from the one in Appendix II due to rounding off. The number of companies for each ISIC category is provided in the table together with (in brackets) the relative contribution from each ISIC category to the domestic manufacturing value added.

groups to domestic value added increased over the period 1982-1992, implying increased knowledge contribution. However, knowledge intensity within the top-ten group remained unchanged (38%).

In Norway, ISIC 31 and 38 increased their share of manufacturing value added, while ISIC 35 decreased its share. The number of knowledge-intensive companies in the top-ten group decreased, but the knowledge contribution of the top-ten group nonetheless rose by 1.4 percentage points. In 1992, the Norwegian knowledge contribution was the highest among the Nordic top-ten groups. However, when the higher degree of concentration is taken into account, knowledge intensity within the Norwegian top-ten group actually decreased slightly.

In Sweden, ISIC 38 was still dominant in 1992, with five companies among the top ten. This was, however, a significant reduction in absolute numbers from 1982 when eight of the ten companies represented this product category. Furthermore, as opposed to 1982, when only three activity groups were represented on the list, as many as six were represented in 1992 (ISIC 31, 33, 34, 35, 37 and 38). This reveals a clear tendency towards a manufacturing industry with a distinctly decreasing knowledge contribution as well as activity concentration. Underlining the tendency, the knowledge intensity of the Swedish industrial core also exhibited a sharp decline (from 83% in 1982 to 60% in 1992).

Hence, our hypothesis about out location of knowledge-intensive activities as a response for outsiders to regionalization has found strong support in the case of Sweden, some support in the case of Norway and no support in the case of Finland. The reason why the decrease has not been larger in the case of Norway and why the knowledge intensity is unchanged in the case of Finland may be that the Finnish and Norwegian manufacturing industries started from an earlier point in the upgrading cycle than the Swedish industries.[50] That is, the Finnish and Norwegian top-ten lists of the mid-1980s contained few knowledge-intensive companies with stakes in the Union market to protect in case of a future Fortress Europe.

V. How Representative is the Sample of Companies?

The reasons for imposing the stock market listing criterion were to increase the probability of acquiring data at the corporate level, as well as to avoid including companies that were state owned and perhaps sheltered from the prevailing market forces and/or not managed in accordance with generally agreed business principles. A crucial question is to what extent this criterion affected the results. Hence, let us here turn to a discussion about the robustness of our findings. Regarding the Danish sample, two large manufacturing companies not listed on the Danish stock exchange were MD Foods (ISIC 31) and Danfoss (ISIC 38). Including these companies on the 1992 top-ten list, the 1992 contribution to domestic value

---

[50] Since the mid-1970s, Swedish manufacturing industries have exhibited one of the highest R&D intensities among the industrial countries: Sweden was for many years second to the United States in terms of industrial R&D expenditures as a percentage of value added (OECD, 1986 and 1992), while the R&D intensities of Denmark, Finland and Norway have been about half of the Swedish intensity. Hence, a clear difference between Sweden and the other Nordic countries existed and still exists in this regard. On a list of the top 200 R&D spenders around the world, fifteen Swedish, three Finnish, one Norwegian and no Danish companies are found in 1993 (Business Week, 1993). In nominal figures, the highest R&D expenditures among the Nordic companies were reported by Volvo (number 19 on the list) and Ericsson (22). Nokia (80) and Hafslund Nycomed (135) were the top R&D companies of Finland and Norway respectively. All these companies represent ISIC categories 35 and 38.

added would be half a percentage point higher than as exhibited in Table 23. Knowledge contribution would be 0.8 percentage points higher. In 1982, only Danfoss would have made the top-ten list. Thus, knowledge contribution over the 1982-1992 period for a top-ten group including Danfoss and MD Foods would have dropped 2.4 percentage points, compared with 1.9 percentage points shown in Table 23. Knowledge intensity would have exhibited an increase of one percentage point. These results support the robustness of our original findings. Companies that would have made the top-ten list according to value added in general, but excluded as being outside the manufacturing sector are AP Möller, Østasiatiske, and Sophus Berendsen, all three conglomerates, the Lauritzen Group in the transportation sector, and Monberg and Thorsen with trading of pharmaceuticals as its main activity. Other candidates were some subsidiaries of foreign groups, such as A/S Dansk Shell, Statoil and Kuwait Petroleum A/S.

The largest Finnish company in terms of sales, chemicals-based Neste, reported sales in 1992 more than twice that of Repola. Neste was, however, not listed on the Finnish stock market and was thus not eligible as a top-ten company in this study. Another large non-listed Finnish company in the chemicals sector was Kemira. Both these companies were 100% state-owned. If the stock market listing criterion were dropped, they would have made the 1982 top-ten list as well as the 1992 top-ten list. The 1992 contribution to domestic value added would only be 0.2 percentage points higher than as exhibited in Table 23, and knowledge contribution would have experienced an increase of three percentage points between 1982 and 1992, as compared with an increase of just over one percentage point as exhibited in Table 23. Hence, the robustness of our results in terms of knowledge contribution is verified. Instead of remaining unchanged, knowledge intensity would have increased slightly. Measured by sales, the non-manufacturing company Kesko was larger than all the Finnish top-ten companies. Kesko, which is a trading company, would probably be on a general value added top-ten list, although, in terms of number of employees, Kesko is much smaller than all the top-ten companies.

In Norway, we found no companies belonging to ISIC categories 31-39 and not listed on the stock market that were large enough to make it on the Norwegian top-ten list. But Statoil, for instance, definitely would have made it on such a list. Its value added contribution was high enough to put it among the top-five companies. However, since it was neither listed on the stock exchange nor a manufacturing company belonging to the relevant ISIC categories, it was not included in this study.

In the case of the Swedish 1992 top-ten list, ABB, whose reported sales were the size of Volvo's and Electrolux's put together, was not considered a Swedish company. Although 50% Swedish and 50% Swiss, from a legal point of view ABB is a Swiss company and therefore not included among the top-ten companies in this study. Another company with close relations to Sweden, but neither considered a Swedish company in 1982 nor in 1992, was Tetra Pak. After the acquisition of Alfa Laval in the fall of 1991, Tetra Laval was formed on 1 January 1993. The Alfa Laval stock was removed from the stock market in October, 1991. Thus, as of the annual report in 1990, financial data for the Alfa Laval concern was not available. However, the consolidated 1992 total value added figures for the company Tetra Pak Alfa Laval indicate that this company would not have made a Swedish top-ten list. A handful of Swedish companies not belonging to category 3 would qualify to be among the top ten companies according to general total value added: Skanska, the largest construction company in Sweden (ISIC classification 5); the KF-group, ICA and Axel Johnsson, trading companies that were among the Swedish top-ten list in terms of sales, and state-owned Televerket.

VI. Conclusions

The dramatic out-flows of FDI in the second half of the 1980s and the beginning of the 1990s changed the core of the manufacturing industries in the Nordic countries, but some patterns registered for the 1982 situation still held true in 1992. For instance, the Swedish top-ten companies remained gigantic in absolute terms as compared with the corresponding companies in the other Nordic countries. However, in many other respects the industrial patterns as reflected in the activities of top-ten companies in Finland, Norway and Sweden have been converging, while the Danish pattern differs. For example, the relative size of total value added of the Finnish, Norwegian and Swedish top-ten groups has converged. So also has contribution to domestic value added. In this respect, in 1992, the Finnish and Norwegian top-ten groups have not only managed to reach the proportion of the Swedish top-ten group, but also to surpass it.

The profile of changes as exhibited by the activities of the top ten manufacturing companies of each country is summarized in Table 24.

Table 24. Nordic national top-ten manufacturing company profiles 1982-92.

	Denmark	Finland	Norway	Sweden
Size of total manufacturing sector as a share of GDP	Unchanged	Decreasing	Decreasing	Decreasing
Real growth as compared to that of the whole domestic manufacturing industry	Lower	Higher	Higher	Lower
Degree of internationalization	Increasing	Increasing	Increasing	Increasing
Degree of activity concentration	Unchanged	Unchanged	Increasing	Decreasing
Degree of size concentration (relative contribution to domestic value added)	Decreasing	Increasing	Increasing	Decreasing
Degree of knowledge contribution to domestic value added	Decreasing	Increasing	Increasing	Decreasing
Degree of knowledge intensity within the top-ten group	Increasing	Unchanged	Decreasing	Decreasing

The Swedish manufacturing core companies experienced a noticeable decrease in knowledge intensity as well as knowledge contribution over the studied period, more than halving the value added contribution of the two knowledge-intensive activity groups to the manufacturing part of GDP. This result is in line with our *a priori* view and is consistent with the findings as reported by Braunerhjelm and Oxelheim (1992, 1994). Due to increased concentration, the knowledge contributions of Norwegian and Finnish top-ten manufacturing companies increased. However, taking the higher degree of concentration into account, knowledge intensity among the Norwegian top-ten companies actually decreased, whereas Finnish knowledge intensity remained unchanged.

A plausible explanation for the strong reaction of the Swedish knowledge-intensive companies, as opposed to that of the Finnish and Norwegian companies, may be that the Swedish manufacturing top-ten companies, at the time they were confronted with the challenge of the EC 1992 Program, were larger and had come further in the upgrading process than their Finnish and Norwegian counterparts. Since they had more or less grown out of the domestic market, their propensity to outsource production was higher than that of the Finnish and Norwegian top-ten manufacturing companies. Moreover, the propensity of the Norwegian knowledge-intensive companies in the petrochemical sector to outsource production may also have been low, since the main natural resource – oil – was, and still is, present and readily available at home. Another explanation for the relatively strong reaction of the Swedish companies may be that the conditions for knowledge-intensive production have been less conducive in Sweden than in Finland and Norway.

According to our hypothesis, the Danish manufacturing industry, as represented by the top-ten manufacturing companies, should have experienced an unchanged, or in a longer perspective, an upgrading of its knowledge contribution and knowledge intensity. The very small increase in knowledge intensity that has been found may partly reflect the fact that, when investment-diverting policies affect companies based in outsider countries, these companies prefer to locate production in insider countries with big markets and/or low production costs. Denmark offered neither of these advantages, and thus received little FDI from its Nordic neighbors or from other outsiders. Moreover, the Danish type of manufacturing specialization offered few network opportunities that could have attracted inward investment.

Over the period from 1982 to 1992, all 40 of the top-ten companies exhibited higher real growth in value added abroad than at home, indicating a strong trend toward internationalization. However, in Finland and Norway, the top-ten companies were still growing faster domestically than the entire domestic manufacturing sector, implying an increasing degree of concentration in these countries. The Finnish and Norwegian top-ten companies are still engines in the domestic growth process. In Denmark and Sweden, a decreasing concentration was registered.

Thus, we have seen some evidence in favor of our *a priori* hypothesis that, in response to the EC 1992 Program, the production pattern of small outsider countries' industries has changed. The industrial sector where this development has been most pronounced in a Nordic context is the Swedish knowledge-intensive, high-income part of the industry. Although some part of this reaction may be traced to domestic sources, the major part is interpreted as being a response to what may have been perceived by Swedish companies as investment diverting policies pursued by the Union authorities. This is only one example of an ongoing race for inward FDI. A race, in which some countries will inevitably become losers. Once the welfare implications have become obvious, there is an impending risk that policy-makers in the concerned outsider countries will try to reimpose capital controls and trigger a global wave of reregulation.

Appendix I

Relative sizes of the Nordic national top-ten companies in 1992

		Denmark	Finland	Norway	Sweden
Average total sales in the top-ten group	MSEK	7,075	16,262	13,949	41,601
Median total sales in the top-ten group	MSEK	5,879	14,003	7,169	36,114
The highest and lowest ranking among the 40 manufacturing companies according to total sales	HIGHEST	20	8	3	1
	LOWEST	40	28	36	18
The highest and lowest ranking according to profits among the 29 manufacturing companies exhibiting profits before tax	HIGHEST	3	9	5	1
	LOWEST	28	29	23	17
The highest and lowest ranking according to loss among the 11 manufacturing companies exhibiting loss before tax	HIGHEST	11	7	5	1
	LOWEST	11	10	6	4
The highest and lowest ranking among the 40 top-ten manufacturing companies according to share of sales abroad	HIGHEST	2	4	3	1
	LOWEST	37	26	40	34
The highest and lowest ranking among the 40 top-ten manufacturing companies according to share of employees abroad	HIGHEST	5	3	4	1
	LOWEST	39	36	40	27
The highest and lowest ranking among the 40 top-ten manufacturing companies according to total number of employees	HIGHEST	21	10	7	1
	LOWEST	40	28	36	25
Average total value added in the top-ten group	MSEK	2,531	5,961	4,681	14,437
Median total value added in the top-ten group	MSEK	1,728	5,083	2,739	13,583
The highest and lowest ranking among the 40 top-ten manufacturing companies according to total value added	HIGHEST	18	8	5	1
	LOWEST	40	27	36	12
The highest and lowest ranking among the 40 top-ten manufacturing companies according to total value added share of total sales	HIGHEST	2	7	1	4
	LOWEST	39	30	38	40
Average domestic value added in the top-ten group	MSEK	1,476	3,389	2,604	5,879
Median domestic value added in the top-ten group	MSEK	1,079	3,289	1,587	5,350
The highest and lowest ranking among the 40 top-ten manufacturing companies according to domestic value added	HIGHEST	12	7	3	1
	LOWEST	40	34	39	26
The highest and lowest ranking among the 40 top-ten manufacturing companies according to domestic value added share of total sales	HIGHEST	1	5	7	9
	LOWEST	37	39	36	40

Appendix II

The ten largest Danish manufacturing companies according to value added in 1992.

1	2	3		4		5	6		7	8
Total value added Rank 1992 (1982)	Group	Value added in millions of DKK, 1992 Current prices		Value added in millions of DKK, 1982 Current prices		Value added in Denmark rank 1992 (rank 1982 within top group 1992)	Value added contribution to the manufacturing part of the Danish GDP (%)		ISIC	Main products
		Total;	in Denmark	Total;	in Denmark		1992	1982		
1(4)	Novo	5,833	4,236	1,443	1,154	1(4)	3.0	1.5	35	Biochemicals
2(3)	Danisco	4,958	2,299	2,053	1,950	2(3)	1.6	2.6	31	Food processing
3(1)	Carlsberg	4,491	2,245	2,828	2,076	3(2)	1.6	2.7	31	Food processing
4(2)	FLS Industries	3,468	1,491	2,831	2,157	4(1)	1.1	2.8	38	Machinery
5(7)	NKT	1,965	1,352	602	572	5(8)	1.0	0.8	38	Electronics
6(5)	Superfos	1,618	883	1,215	1,057	7(5)	0.6	1.4	35	Chemicals
7(9)	Jens Villadsen	1,105	278	552	145	10(10)	0.2	0.2	36	Goods from minerals
8(8)	Aalborg Portland	961	886	581	581	6(7)	0.6	0.8	36	Goods from minerals
9(-)	Royal Copenhagen	932	814	264	240	9(-)	0.6	0.3	36	Goods from minerals
10(-)	Bang & Olufsen	911	825	395	343	8(-)	0.6	0.4	38	Electronics
	Total for the 1992 top-ten group	26,242	15,309	12,764	10,275		10.9	13.5		
	The total contribution to Danish GDP from the manufacturing industries in Denmark (current prices)	141,850								
	Real growth in total domestic manufacturing value added in Denmark						55,4			

Real growth rates have been deflated with wholesale price indices 1982-1992.
The 1982 figures as well as all real growth figures for Royal Copenhagen are estimates.

Appendix III

The ten largest Finnish manufacturing companies according to value added in 1992.

1	2	3		4		5	6		7	8
Total value added Rank 1992 (1982)	Group	Value added in millions of FIM, 1992 Current prices		Value added in millions of FIM, 1982 Current prices		Value added in Finland rank 1992 (rank 1982 within top group 1992)	Value added contribution to the manufacturing part of the Finnish GDP (%)		ISIC	Main products
		Total;	in Finland	Total;	in Finland		1992	1982		
1(3)	Repola	8,557	5,182	1,843	1,788	1(3)	5.6	3.1	33.34	Wood, pulp and paper
2(1)	Nokia	6,075	3,121	2,703	2,216	4(1)	3.4	3.9	38	Electronics
3(-)	Outokumpu	5,213	2,494	1,188	1,150	6(-)	2.7	2.0	38	Metal products
4(4)	Kymmene	4,884	3,658	1,801	1,839	2(4)	4.0	3.2	33.34	Wood, pulp and paper
5(6)	Kone	3,972	622	1,563	547	10(10)	0.7	1.0	38	Machinery
6(-)	Valmet	3,848	2,565	1,294	1,151	5(-)	2.8	2.0	38	Machinery
7(2)	Enso-Gutzeit	3,843	3,159	2,061	1,855	3(2)	3.4	3.2	33.34	Wood, pulp and paper
8(5)	Metra	3,744	1,033	1,800	1,620	9(5)	1.1	2.8	38	Machinery
9(9.10)	Metsä-Serla	2,930	2,078	1,681	1,614	8(7,9)	2.2	2.8	33.34	Wood, pulp and paper
10(-)	Rautaruukki	2,782	2,157	1,162	1,148	7(-)	2.3	2.0	37	Iron & steel
Total for the 1992 top-ten group		45,849	26,068	17,096	14,928		28.2	26.0		
The total contribution to Finnish GDP from the manufacturing industries in Finland (current prices)			92,432							
Real growth in total domestic manufacturing value added in Finland						22,8				

Real growth rates have been deflated with wholesale price indices 1982-1992.
Metsä-Serla is the result of a merger between G.A. Serlachius and Metsäliiton Teollisuus.

Appendix IV

The ten largest Norwegian manufacturing companies according to value added in 1992.

1	2	3		4		5	6		7	8
Total value added Rank 1992 (1982)	Group	Value added in millions of NOK, 1992 Current prices		Value added in millions of NOK, 1982 Current prices		Value added in Norway rank 1992 (rank 1982 within top group 1992)	Value added contribution to the manufacturing part of the Norwegian GDP (%)		ISIC	Main products
		Total;	in Norway	Total;	in Norway		1992	1982		
1(1)	Norsk Hydro	17,327	8,478	7,087	3,756	1(1)	9.0	7.3	35	Chemicals, petrochem.
2(2)	Kvaerner	7,565	3,199	1,831	1,794	4(2)	3.4	3.5	38	Machinery
3(4)	Aker	6,131	4,425	1,161	987	3(5)	4.7	1.9	38	Machinery
4(10)	Orkla	5,703	4,602	402	358	2(10)	4.9	0.7	31	Food processing
5(-)	Hafslund Nycomed	3,273	1,509	2,828	2,076	6(-)	1.6	4.0	35	Pharmaceuticals
6(9)	Dyno	2,579	641	563	512	10(8)	0.7	1.0	35	Chemicals
7(-)	Freia Marabou	2,263	752	223	149	9(-)	0.8	0.3	31	Food processing
8(3)	Elkem	1,997	1,498	1,659	1,261	7(3)	1.6	2.5	37	Iron, steel, non-ferrous metals
9(8)	Norske Skogsindustrier	1,925	1,881	635	629	5(7)	2.0	1.2	33,34	Wood, pulp and paper
10(-)	Rieber & Son	1,232	833	218	208	8(-)	0.9	0.4	31	Food processing
	Total for the 1992 top-ten group	49,995	27,819	16,607	11,730		29.6	22.8		
	The total contribution to Norwegian GDP from the manufactoring industries in Norway (current prices)	94,281								
	Real growth in total domestic manufacturing value added in Norway					6,3				

Real growth rates have been deflated with wholesale price indices 1982-1992.

Appendix V

The ten largest Swedish manufacturing companies according to value added in 1992.

1	2	3		4		5	6		7	8
Total value added Rank 1992 (1982)	Group	Value added in millions of SEK, 1992 Current prices		Value added in millions of SEK, 1982 Current prices		Value added in Sweden rank 1992 (rank 1982 within top group 1992)	Value added contribution to the manufacturing part of the Swedish GDP (%)		ISIC	Main products
		Total;	in Sweden	Total;	in Sweden		1992	1982		
1 (2)	Electrolux	26,417	3,533	12,187	4,485	7 (5)	1.4	3.5	38	Machinery
2 (3)	Ericsson	18,129	7,746	10,751	4,623	4 (4)	3.1	3.6	38	Electronics
3 (1)	Volvo	17,294	11,251	13,653	10,239	1 (1)	4.4	7.9	38	Transport equipment
4 (-)	Procordia	16,861	10,065	4,081	3,568	2 (-)	4.0	2.8	31	Food processing
5 (-)	Stora	15,208	7,166	1,984	1,696	6 (-)	2.8	1.3	33.34	Wood, pulp and paper
6 (5)	SKF	11,958	1,760	7,780	1,735	10 (10)	0.7	1.3	38	Machinery
7 (-)	SCA	11,069	3,385	2,378	1,557	8 (-)	1.3	1.2	33.34	Wood, pulp and paper
8 (6)	Saab-Scania	10,753	7,313	6,837	5,606	5 (3)	2.9	4.3	38	Transport equipment
9 (8)	Sandvik	8,368	3,128	4,312	3,622	3 (6)	1.2	2.8	37	Iron, steel products
10 (-)	Astra	8,316	3,442	1,401	1,296	9 (-)	1.4	1.0	35	Pharmaceuticals
Total for the 1992 top-ten group		144,373	58,789	65,364	38,427		23.2	29.7		
	The total contribution to Swedish GDP from the manufactoring industries in Sweden (current prices)	253,000								
	Real growth in total domestic manufacturing value added in Sweden					23,2				

Real growth rates have been deflated with producer price indices 1982-1992 within category 3 according to ISIC.

References

Braunerhjelm, P. and L. Oxelheim (1992): *Heckscher-Ohlin and Schumpeter Industries: The Response by Swedish Multinational Firms to the EC 1992 Program. Working Paper 352.* Stockholm: Industrial Institute for Economic and Social Research.

Braunerhjelm, P. and L. Oxelheim (1994): Structural Implications of the Investment Response by Swedish Multinational Firms to the EC 1992 Program. *Working Paper 1994/5.* Lund: Institute of Economic Research.

Business Week (1993): The Global 1000, July 12.

Eliasson, G., Fölster, S., Lindberg, T., Pousette, T. and Taymaz, E. (1990): *The Knowledge Based Information Economy.* Stockholm: Industrial Institute for Social and Economic Research.

Heum, P. and P. Ylä-Anttila in cooperation with P. Braunerhjelm and S. Thomsen (1992): *Firm Dynamics in a Nordic Perspective – Large Corporations and Industrial Transformation.* Helsinki: Taloustieto Oy.

Hirsch, S. and S. Thomsen (1993): Large Industrial Firms in Small Economies. *Working Paper 3-93.* Copenhagen: Institute for International Economy and Management.

OECD (1992): *International Direct Investments: Policies and Trends in the 1980s.* Paris: OECD.

OECD (1986, 1992): *OECD Science and Technology Indicators* (various issues). Paris: OECD.

Oxelheim, L. (1984): The Largest Nordic Manufacturing Companies, in DØR, ETLA, IUI and IØI, *Economic Growth in a Nordic Perspective.* Helsinki:

Oxelheim, L. (1993): Foreign Direct Investment and the Liberalization of Capital Movements, in Oxelheim, L. (ed.) *The Global Race for Foreign Direct Investment.* Berlin: Springer-Verlag.

Oxelheim, L. (1995): *Financial Markets in Transition - Globalization, Investment and Economic Growth.* London: Routledge.

Oxelheim, L. and R. Gärtner (1994): Small Country Manufacturing Industries in Transition – the Case of the Nordic Region. *Management International Review 4*: Gabler Verlag, Vol. 34, 1994/4 pp. 331-356.

Chapter 6:
European Integration and Uruguay Round Results on Trade in Services

New challenges for the Swiss economy

Philippe Gugler

Services are playing an increasingly important role in the economies of all industrialized and most developing countries. Services account for about 60-70 % of GDP and employment in OECD countries and represent about 20% of world trade and almost 50% of annual flows of foreign direct investment.

Given the considerable importance of services in the world economy as well as in international economic relations, services have become a more and more important issue in international economic policy (Gaudard 1989). For the first time, services have been negotiated under the auspices of the GATT in the context of the Uruguay Round negotiation of the General Agreement on Trade in Services (GATS). Though regional agreements previously concentrated on goods, agreements to liberalize international transactions in services have been prominent in the late 1980s and early 1990s (Canada-USA Free Trade Agreement, NAFTA, EC92, EEA, Australia-New Zealand Closer Economic Relation trade agreement, etc.).

Services are playing an important role in Switzerland where they represent about 60% of the economy (in terms of share of GDP as well as in terms of numbers of employees and numbers of firms). Furthermore, the current account surplus registered by the Swiss service sector has compensated for the traditional deficit of Swiss trade balance for many years.

Switzerland is considered to be a small country. It can be argued that foreign trade is of greater weight in the economic activity of a small country – such as Switzerland – than in that of a larger country. According to Kutnets (1960, p. 18), "this is particularly true of nations that have developed and attained fairly high levels of per capita output and consumption". As indicated by Scitovsky (1960), international trade and/or economic integration are of tremendous importance for small countries because they "can offset the disadvantages of smallness in the economic sense".

For Switzerland, a country that does not participate in the European Economic Area (EEA) and is not a member of the European Union, the Uruguay Round Negotiation's results are of great importance in order to preserve market access and national treatment of its firms abroad, particularly in the Union, which is the major market for Swiss firms.

Taking into account the case of Switzerland and of the level of internationalization of Swiss firms, this chapter focuses on the interrelationship between two major developments: first, the EC92 program, particularly in the service sector, and its discriminatory measures *vis-à-vis* non-Union countries such as Switzerland; second, the role of GATS in reducing discriminatory treatment of non-Union countries in the service sector.

I. The Internationalization of Swiss Firms

Regionalism and multilateralism of trade are of great importance for Switzerland, whose economy is highly linked to world trade. Table 25 shows that the share of Swiss exports and imports in the GDP have increased during recent decades: exports of goods and services account for 36% of GDP whereas imports of goods and services represent 32.5% of GDP (1992). Swiss foreign direct investment (FDI) is important compared with the level of domestic activities: for example, in 1991 the 50 largest employers were employing 526,056 people within Switzerland, whereas they were employing 1,016,262 people abroad (Handelszeitung 1992).

Swiss international business is highly linked with the Union. In 1993, Swiss exports to and imports from the Union represented 57% and 74% of total exports and imports (OECD 1994).

The EC92 internal market has induced an increase in the Swiss FDI and the FDI of many other non-member countries in the Union (Table 26). Indeed, the massive inflow of FDI into the Union since the late 1980s suggests that firms expect the beneficial impact of the internal market to accrue predominantly to insiders (Hirsch and Almor 1992; Braunerhjelm and Oxelheim 1993). As indicated by Dunning (1993a), "more generally, the completion of the internal market will most certainly affect the relative competitiveness of EC firms vis-à-vis non-EC firms and the attractions of a European location for investment by all kinds of firms". The fear of

Table 25. Swiss exports and imports of goods and services (1950-1992) as a percentage of GDP (Nominal).

Year	Share of exports	Share of imports
1950	25.2	26.3
1960	29.3	29.6
1970	32.8	34.5
1980	36.7	40.3
1990	3.9	36.4
1992	36.0	32.5

Source: Swiss National Bank

being excluded from a potential growth market seems to be one of the major determinants of the inflows of investments from outsider firms into the Union (Dunning, 1988). The internal market of the Union seems to have influenced the allocation of FDI of many countries, including Switzerland.

A shift in locational advantages affects different firms in different ways. (Dunning 1993b). We observed the effects of the EC92 program on the allocation of Swiss FDI by separating firms into two major categories: manufacturing and service firms.

The following developments were observed (Table 27):[51]

- *The accumulated flow of FDI in the Union between 1985 and 1987 was smaller than the accumulated flow of FDI in the Union between 1988 and 1990.*

  In 1987, the Single Act was approved by the Union countries. Since this created the possibility that outsiders might experience locational disadvantages, Swiss firms reacted to the new market situation by increasing their volume of investments within the Union.

- *The ratio of accumulated flow of FDI between the Union and North America for 1985-1987 was smaller than the ratio of accumulated flow of FDI between the Union and North America for 1988-1992.*

  North America was the other main recipient of Swiss FDI, and the growth of the North America market in 1985-1987 was strong; whereas Europe suffered from "Eurosclerosis". Thus investments in the United States were large during this period. However, the differences

---

[51] Statistics before 1985 were not available.

Table 26. Flows of Swiss FDI (industry and services), 1985-1992.

Swiss FDI in industry (in millions of CHF)

Region	1985	1986	1987	1988	1989	1990	1991	1992
EFTA	111	13	130	208	1,205	-352	747	352
European Community	2,866	555	855	7,263	2,120	2,388	1,978	2,784
Middle and eastern Europe	-25	-19	0	-5	20	17	64	146
Rest of Europe	3	22	17	113	41	36	-52	52
North America	6,416	232	1,055	-135	2,861	-53	92	1,289
Latin America	685	596	-207	1,483	941	2,578	1,420	1,434
Middle East	17	33	-88	-24	104	-117	44	16
Africa	-3	47	24	70	29	105	156	75
Australia, New Zealand	0	150	-29	167	27	221	75	142
Asia, Oceania	516	278	37	-24	166	273	195	849
Total	*10,584	*1,906	*1,795	9,116	*7,512	5,096	4,719	7,139

Swiss FDI in services (in millions of CHF)

Region	1985	1986	1987	1988	1989	1990	1991	1992
EFTA	-1	6	-9	79	37	80	105	-88
European Community	348	473	1,510	1,453	966	2,134	2,624	1,348
Middle and eastern Europe	1	1	1	-1	-1	2	2	2
Rest of Europe	2	-2	7	-21	52	2	-17	-26
North America	180	8	-1,480	1,362	3,057	199	1,264	-48
Latin America	32	177	-34	463	861	924	368	-560
Middle East	14	-33	3	100	104	19	0	2
Africa	-42	-27	5	-2	11	-19	37	8
Australia, New Zealand	0	10	32	121	83	77	143	108
Asia, Oceania	23	109	69	52	163	336	137	89
Total	*558	*721	*105	*3,607	*5,331	*3,753	*4,662	835

Swiss FDI in industry & services
(in millions of CHF)

Region	1985	1986	1987	1988	1989	1990	1991	1992
EFTA	110	18	121	287	1,241	-273	852	264
European Community	3,214	1,028	2,365	8,716	3,085	4,521	4,601	4,132
Middle and eastern Europe	-25	-18	2	-5	19	19	66	148
Rest of Europe	5	20	24	93	94	37	-69	26
North America	6,596	240	-425	1,227	5,917	146	1,355	1,241
Latin America	717	773	-241	1,946	1,802	3,502	1,788	874
Middle East	31	0	-85	76	208	-98	44	18
Africa	-45	20	28	68	39	86	193	83
Australia, New Zealand	0	160	4	288	110	298	218	250
Asia, Oceania	539	387	105	28	328	609	332	938
Total	*11,143	*2,627	*1,899	12,724	12,843	*8,848	*9,381	7,974

*Error due to rounding
Source: Swiss National Bank

between FDI in the Union and in the United States have diminished since 1987. There was a relative increase in FDI in the Union over the latter period.

- *The ratio of accumulated flow of FDI between the Union and the rest of the world for 1985-1987 was smaller than ratio of accumulated flow of FDI between the Union and the rest of the world for 1988-1992.*

There was a relative increase of FDI in the Union over the later period.

- *The services/manufacturing ratio of accumulated flow of FDI in the Union for 1985-1987 was smaller than the services/manufacturing ratio of accumulated flow of FDI in the Union for 1988-1992.*

We may attribute this fact to the relative locational disadvantages experienced by Swiss firms, which seem more important in the service sector than in the manufacturing sector for two main reasons. First, since 1972 free trade agreements were signed between Switzerland and the Union in the goods sectors, whereas such agreements have not existed in the service sector. Second, progress toward the achievement of an internal market has been more pronounced in services than in goods. Since 1957, most liberalization developments have occurred in the manufacturing sector rather than in the service sector.

According to a study that relies on 510 strategic alliances identified since 1982 by Handelszeitung (Kern 1994), Swiss firms are increasingly entering into strategic alliances with domestic and foreign partners. The EC92 internal market seems to have influenced the allocation of foreign partners of Swiss firms (Tables 28, 29-30).

According to the data available (Table 31),[52] the following developments were observed :

- *The ratio of the accumulated strategic alliances in Switzerland to the accumulated number of strategic alliances abroad between 1982 and 1986 was greater than the same ratio for 1988-1992*

Before the mid-1980s, international strategic alliances were not a common way of doing business abroad. However, since the mid-1980s, international strategic alliances have been numerous (Gugler and Dunning 1994, Gugler, 1992). We observed the same evolution as far as Swiss firms are concerned.

- *The ratio of the accumulated number of strategic alliances in Switzerland to the accumulated number of strategic alliances in the Union between 1982 and 1986 was greater than the same ratio for 1988-1992.*

---

[52] Statistics for 1987 were not available. In fact, we have only statistics for strategic alliances between Swiss firms and European Firms and not between Swiss firms and Union firms. However, according to sectoral studies, we may postulate that the majority of European partners are Union firms.

Table 27. Trends in Swiss FDI, (1985-1992).

	1985-1987	1988-1992
Accumulated flow of FDI in the European Community	6,607	16,322 a
European Community/ North American ratio of accumulated flow of FDI	0.9	1.9
European Community/ rest of the world ratio of accumulated flow of FDI	0.7	0.9
Services/manufacturing ratio of accumulated flow of FDI in the EC	0.3	0.8

a) 1988-1990

Table 28. Swiss strategic alliances by sectors (number) and years (1982-1992).

Sector	82	83	84	85	86	88	89	90	91	91
Machinery	4	2	7	2	3	12	11	18	9	12
Chemical	1	1	3	4	6	5	11	9	13	8
Electronic	0	2	2	4	5	7	14	10	4	12
Transport	0	0	0	3	3	3	7	7	5	6
Consulting	0	1	1	2	1	2	5	9	6	7
Food	1	1	0	0	3	0	7	9	2	9
Banking	0	1	1	0	3	2	5	5	8	4
Audiovisual	0	1	0	1	0	4	2	5	4	5
Metal products	1	1	2	1	3	1	1	3	5	0
Insurance	0	0	0	1	1	0	2	5	3	4
Construction	1	3	0	1	0	0	0	4	2	5
Distribution	2	1	0	2	2	1	1	0	2	4
Beverages	0	1	0	0	0	0	3	3	5	3
Textile	2	3	0	0	1	2	2	2	3	0
Software	0	1	0	1	5	0	3	1	0	2

Source: Stephan Kern, *Eine empirische Studie über strategische Allianzen von Schweizer Unternehmungen*, University of Berne 1994.

Table 29. Swiss strategic alliances by sectors and geographical areas (number), 1982-1992.

Sector	Switzerland	Europe	North America	Asia	Other
Machinery	28	34	9	9	0
Chemical	11	12	24	11	3
Electronic	22	20	13	4	1
Transport	13	14	2	5	0
Consulting	12	18	2	1	1
Food	17	7	3	4	1
Banking	10	13	2	3	1
Audiovisual	16	6	0	0	0
Metal products	8	8	2	0	0
Insurance	8	6	0	1	1
Construction	11	3	2	0	0
Distribution	6	7	0	1	1
Beverages	10	4	1	0	0
Textile	10	4	1	0	0
Software	9	3	0	0	1

Source: Stephan Kern, *Eine empirische Studie über strategische Allianzen von Schweizer Unternehmungen*, University of Berne 1994.

The relative number of strategic alliances concluded between Swiss and Union firms compared with the relative number of strategic alliances concluded between Swiss firms has increased in recent years, due both to the global increase of international strategic alliances versus national strategic alliances and to the attraction of Union firms as partners because of the EC 1992 internal market program.

- *The ratio of the accumulated number of strategic alliances in the Union to the accumulated number of strategic alliances in North America between 1982 and 1988 was smaller than the same ratio for 1988-1992.*

This trend was due mainly to the attraction of the 1992 internal market within the Union.

- *The ratio of the number of accumulated strategic alliances in the Union to the*

Table 30. Swiss strategic alliances by years and geographical areas (number)
1982-1992.

Region	1982	1983	1984	1985	1986	1988	1989	1990	1991	1992
Switzerland	8	15	13	15	21	14	29	36	20	40
Europe	7	4	1	6	8	8	28	39	44	38
North America	0	1	2	4	5	9	14	10	9	10
Asia	1	2	1	1	3	7	10	8	6	2
Other	0	0	0	0	1	1	4	3	1	1

Source: Stephan Kern, *Eine empirische Studie über strategische Allianzen von Schweizer Unternehmungen*, University of Berne 1994.

number of accumulated strategic alliances in the rest of the world between 1982 and 1988 was smaller than the same ratio for 1988-1992.

This trend was due mainly to the attraction of the 1992 internal market within the Union.

- *The ratio of the strategic alliances in industry to the strategic alliances in services between 1982 and 1986 was greater than the same ratio for 1988 and 1992.*

As internationalization of services grows, for example, FDI in services, it is not surprising that the increase of strategic alliances in services is more important than the increase of strategic alliances in the industry sector.

The impact of the EC92 program on the distribution of Swiss FDI and Swiss international strategic alliances is significant, particularly in the service sector. This is due mainly to the influence of the EC92 program on locational advantage, which creates an incentive for foreign firms to invest within the Union and/or to conclude strategic alliances with Union firms. The importance of the locational advantages depends on the level of discrimination affecting non-member country firms. This level reflects the gap between the degree of liberalization within the Union and the degree of liberalization contracted under the GATS by the Union towards third countries.

Table 31. Comparison of Swiss strategic alliances, 1982-1992.

	1982-1988 a	1989-1992
Strategic alliances in Switzerland/ **Strategic alliances Abroad**	1.6	0.55
Strategic alliances in Switzerland/ **Strategic alliances in Europe**[b]	2.8	0.88
Strategic alliances in Europe/ **Strategic alliances in North America**	2.2	3.0
Strategic alliances in Europe/ **Strategic alliances in the rest of the world**[c]	1.2	1.6
Strategic alliances in Industry/ **Strategic alliances in Services**	2.3	1.6

a) Data for 1987 not available.
b) Data for the European Community are not available, but according to several sectoral statistics, it can be argued that the strategic alliances with non-EC firms constitutes a minority of cases in the total number of strategic alliances with European firms.
c) Strategic alliances in the rest of the world: strategic alliances concluded with foreign enterprises minus strategic alliances concluded with the ECís firms.

II. EC92 on Services

The main objective of the Treaty of Rome is the realization of the four freedoms of free internal movement of goods, services, labor and capital (including the right of establishment). In principle, no restrictions exist on intra-Union movement of services and goods, according to the White Paper. Natural and judicial bodies that are Union members have the right to become established in any Union country. Although the free movement of services and the right of establishment were integral parts of the original Treaty of Rome, progress towards creating effective free trade in services was rather slow until the mid-1980s. However, The EC92 program has far-reaching potential in terms of liberalizing intra-Union service markets. The various Union directives relating specifically to services as well as those relating to competition policy are likely to induce major changes in all service sectors in the Union over the next several years (Ruane 1990).

The EC92 proposals to ensure free internal trade of services include specific directives covering four areas: financial services (banking, insurance, securities, mortgage lending, and investment services); transport services (air, maritime, and road transport); miscellaneous sectors (tourism, engineering, broadcasting, medical practice, legal services, management consultancy and accountancy); and cross-sectoral directives (government procurement). Liberalization of trade in services calls for liberalization in the movement of people. The EC92 program contains proposals to allow the free movement of people within the Union, focusing on the elimination of obstacles to labor and the professions. The directives include mutual recognition of higher educational diplomas, medical training, technical training and elimination of burdensome residential permit requirements (Gugler, 1993).

Three basic elements to be considered in the EC92 approach to liberalize trade in services are:

- abolition of discriminatory measures concerning trade and establishment
- mutual recognition and home-country control
- minimum harmonization of rules

Since the announcement of the 1992 program, the threat of Fortress Europe has created major concern. Words like reciprocity, transition strategy and infant industry strategy raise the specter of Fortress Europe in some specific sectors such as in financial services and telecommunication (the Naisbitt Group). The main questions raised by EC92 are based on the discriminatory potential against third countries.

For Switzerland, six scenarios of integration have been considered, resulting from the following choices:

(1) The choice between:
   (a) maintenance of the existing national legislation (domestic status quo), which means no adaptation of Swiss legislation to the European Union or EEA legislation; or
   (b) adjustment of the Swiss legislation to European Union or EEA legislation.

(2) The choice between:
- (A) Dissociation from the Union/EEA (that is, Switzerland stays outside the Union and the EEA);
- (B) Participation of Switzerland in the EEA Treaty; or
- (C) Union membership of Switzerland.

Since the scenarios (Ba) and (Ca) are not feasible (neither under the EEA Treaty nor under the Union membership would Switzerland be allowed to maintain status quo in its legislation), four scenarios remained to be considered as shown in Table 32: (Aa, Ab, Bb and Cb). As the Swiss population rejected the EEA Treaty on 6 December 1992, the scenarios linked to the (B) option (participation of Switzerland in the EEA Treaty) as well as the scenarios linked to the (C) option (Union membership of Switzerland) seem to be unfeasible in the near future. However, since they can not be excluded they must still be considered to be options.

Even if Switzerland followed the (Aa) option (dissociation and maintenance of the status quo), two regulatory adjustments – already decided – would be in force.

First, there is the transit agreement with the Union on road transport. This agreement stipulates the removal of several Swiss restrictions concerning width and length of trucks allowed on Swiss roads. Second, the insurance agreement between Switzerland and the Union for non-life business insurance stipulates the absence of discrimination between established insurance companies and insurance companies that are becoming established in the Union and Switzerland.

The (Ab) scenario would require important reforms. Concerning the (Bb) and (Cb) scenarios, according to Zweifel, "in the short run, signing the EEA Treaty and EC membership have the same regulatory implications for the service industries studied, with the partial exception of immigration policy. In the long run, the important difference lies in an EC member's potential influence on EC decisions especially with regard to technological standards" (Zweifel 1993).

Apart form the regulatory adjustments (summarized in Table 32), induced structural adjustments by the Swiss economy have to be taken into account. For the time being, the (Ab) scenario seems to prevail. In this context, Switzerland, as well as the other non-member countries, may have been suffering from the disparity between conditions offered within the Union to European Union Member states and EEA members as com-

Table 32. Required regulatory adjustments under four scenarios. [a)b]

Criteria	(A) Dissociation	(B) EEA treaty	(C) European Union membership
(a) Maintenance of domestic current legislation	Implementation of transit Agreement (road transport) Implement of Insurance Agreement (Nonlife)	***Scenario not feasible***	***Scenario not feasible***
(b) Adjustment of domestic regulation to Union legislation	• Market allocation of immigrant labor • Freedom of ownership or real estate for foreigners • Liberalization of public procurement (construction) • Full implementation of open network provision (telecommunication) • Freedom of cabotage (road transport) • Liberalization of opening hours (retail trade) • Tradeable permits for locations of shopping centers (retail trade) • Full disclosure and dissemination of information (banking, insurance) • Freedom of services (life insurance) • Free combination of lines of business (insurance) • Abolition of license for restaurant (tourism)	• Liberalization of immigration with escape clause [x+5] • Freedom of ownership of real estate for foreigners • Liberalization of public procurement (construction) [1989] • Full implementation of open network provision (telecommunication) [1996] • Liberalization of voice telephony [1996 or later] • Liberalization of Sunday and night circulation (road transport) [x] • Non-subsidization of combined mode (road transport) [x] • Freedom of cabotage [1996] • Single license (banking, insurance) [x] • Home control (banking, insurance) [x] • Full disclosure in accounting (banking) • Appeal to exemptions from anti-cartel provisions (insurance) • Implementation of consumer protection (tourism)	• Full liberalization of immigration [x+?] • Freedom of ownership of real estate for foreigners • Liberalization of public procurement (construction) [1989] • Full implementation of open network provision (telecommunication) [1996] • Liberalization of telephony [1996 or later] • Liberalization of Sunday and night circulation (road transport) [x] • Non-subsidization of combined mode (road transport) [x] • Freedom of cabotage [1996] • Single license (banking, insurance) [x] • Home control (banking, insurance) [x] • Full disclosure in accounting (banking) • Appeal to exemptions from anti-cartel provisions (insurance)

Source: P. Zweifel (ed.), Services in Switzerland: Structure, Performance, and Implications of European Economic Integration. Berlin: Springer Verlag, 1993.

[a)] Affected service industries in parentheses
[b)] Time of implementation in brackets; x = Time of ratification/accession

pared with the conditions offered to non-members by Union trade policy. As indicated by Zweifel, "there is some empirical evidence suggesting that Swiss merchandise exports into large EC countries have been hampered by non-tariff barriers to a particular high degree. To the extent that the EC will adhere to a 'large country' common foreign trade policy, Switzerland may thus be exposed to increasing non-tariff barriers acting on its direct exports of services" (Zweifel 1993).

As regulatory and structural adjustments by Switzerland seem not to be sufficient in order to compensate for the disadvantages of being outside the Union, the Uruguay Round negotiations in trade in services are of tremendous importance in order to reduce potential and current Union discriminatory threats.

III. The General Agreement on Trade in Services (GATS)

The eighth round of multilateral negotiations, launched in Punta del Este in September 1986 under the auspices of the GATT, was concluded on December 15, 1993. For the first time, liberalization of trade in services has been formally placed on the multilateral negotiating agenda in order to achieve a General Agreement on Trade in Services (GATS)[53], which is an integral part of the Uruguay Round's results.

The GATS covers all services and applies to all measures affecting all modes of delivery[54] of trade in services. This Agreement is based on three pillars: the general obligations and principles, the national initial commitments (schedule concessions)[55] and a set of sectoral annexes and other attachments:

- *General obligations*

General obligations are stated in Parts I and II of the framework, which aims at achieving progressively higher levels of liberalization of trade in services, and at providing more predictability and stability in this trade. The most important ones are:

---

[53] See Appendix I for the content of the GATS.
[54] Four modes of delivery of services are distinguished in the GATS (see Table 33).
[55] The Final Act contains Ministerial Decisions with regard to negotiation on basic telecommunications, maritime transport and labor mobility which will be held during the following months for a period of time indicated in each of these Decisions.

- *Most-Favored-Nation Treatment (Article II):*

Article II is a core general obligation of the GATS. It requires every GATS member to offer, unconditionally, treatment no less favorable than is accorded for similar services or service suppliers from another member country. As indicated by Hoekman 1992, "this implies that once the GATS enters into force, any measures that do discriminate across different foreign suppliers would violate the agreement, unless a temporary exception has been sought for the nonconforming measure".

- *Transparency (Article III)*

According to Article III, all laws and regulations should be made public and easily accessible to all service providers.

- *Increasing Participation of Developing Countries (Article IV)*

This article provides for flexibility in the initial application of rules in order to permit developing countries time to assume obligations.

- *Economic Integration (Article V)*

This article allows economic integration under certain conditions.

- *Domestic Regulation (Article VI)*

According to Article VII, in sectors where commitments are undertaken, each member shall ensure that all measures affecting trade in services are administered in a reasonable, objective and impartial manner.

- *Recognition of Licenses and Certification (Article VII)*

This article calls for the establishment of procedures for the recognition of licenses, education and experience granted by a specific member.

- *Specific Commitments*

Part III of the framework contains three articles entitled Market Access (Article XVI), National Treatment (Article XVII) and Additional Commitments (Article XVIII). These articles are not general but apply only to the service sector and subsectors where commitments to offer market access and national treatment have been undertaken by members. These specific commitments on market access and national treatment apply to the service sector and sub-sectors and are listed in a positive manner in a member's schedule, subject to horizontal (cross-sectoral) and/or sector-specific qualifications or condition, if any. A schedule of commitments is required of each member intending to sign the GATS. These commitments bind members to ensure that national regulatory regimes are consistent with the schedules in regard to the sectors and subsectors to which they apply.

Article XVI states that "with respect to market access through the modes of supply identified in Article I, each member shall accord services and service providers of other member treatment no less favorable than that provided for under the terms, limitations and conditions agreed and specified in its schedule". In sectors or subsectors where market access commitments are undertaken, a member shall not maintain: (i) quantitative restrictions (for example, limitations on the number of service providers); (ii) and/or measures that restrict or require a specific type of legal entity or joint venture; (iii) and/or a limitation on the participation of foreign capital.

According to Article XVII, national treatment is defined as "treatment no less favorable than it accords to its own like services and service providers". It is stated that the *de jure* standard of national treatment is not sufficient because identical treatment may worsen the conditions of competition for foreign service suppliers (for example, requirement for insurance that reserves must be held in the host country). For this reason, *de facto* national treatment has to be considered, which means that it is necessary to take also into account the potential discriminatory measures, even if they are applied equally to foreign and domestic service suppliers.

The following examples of limitations on national treatment may be mentioned: 1) domestic providers of audiovisual services may be given preference in the allocation of frequencies for transmission within the national territory, and 2) a law may require that access to the accountancy sector is open exclusively to graduates who have accomplished their studies at local universities. These two articles reflect both the distinction between measures that are applied at the border (market access restrictions) and measures that are applied within borders (national treatment) and the fact that international trade in services is often restricted by non-discriminatory measures. In services, we have to recognize that many barriers do not act at the border (cross-border barriers) *but result from domestic regulation.*

The schedule of commitments determines the extent of market access opportunities resulting from the GATS "if most countries list most of their service sectors in their schedules, and do not impose restrictive conditions or limitations on alternative modes of supply, the effective market access opportunities resulting from the Agreement may prove to be substantial. Conversely, if many sectors are excluded (i.e. not listed in country schedules), or if many restrictions are imposed with respect to modes of supply and the application of national treatment and market access in scheduled sectors, the Agreement will have little immediate impact in terms of effective liberalization" (Hoekman and Sauvé 1993).

- *The annexes*

The framework contains six annexes: Article II (Most-Favored-Nation) exemptions and sectoral annexes for financial services, telecommunications, air transport, basic telecommunications, maritime transport, the movement of natural persons providing services covered by the framework: As indicated by Carlisle (1991), "their aim is to interpret or, in some cases, qualify the application of provisions of the main text to take account of the particular characteristics of specific sectors".

According to the GATS, members may not introduce more restrictive measures than those stated in their national schedules, that is, the content of national schedules at the conclusion of the Uruguay Round will represent the effective stage of multilateral liberalization of trade in services. This stage constitutes in fact the initial phase because, according to Article XIX of GATS (progressive liberalization), liberalization of services will continue under the auspices of new rounds of negotiations: existing barriers to service trade should be reduced, a process for ongoing liberalization should be established and no new barriers should be erected.

In fact, the value of the GATS is not only based on national schedules but also on the national Most-Favored-Nation exemptions lists that – like the national specific commitments schedules – have to be negotiated among the Members.

IV. The Role of GATS for Outsiders to EC92

The renewed interest in regionalism has created a concern that the world trade system may increasingly depend on regional blocs allied with the Union, the United States and Japan (Lawson 1992). Some experts argue that the recent trend towards regionalism may carry greater risks of becoming a substitute for (rather than complementary to) multilateralism, whereas others argue that regionalism may promote multilateralism (Bagwati, 1992; Fieleke, 1992; Loyd, 1992). It seems recognized that the risks of regionalism are lower when regional arrangements have an outward orientation. Furthermore, some studies indicate that globalization of investments and production is likely to lessen the risk of regional agreements becoming "closed doors".

The purpose of this chapter is not to deal with the debate over regionalism versus multilateralism, but rather to examine the specific case of EC92 – how it affects the service sectors, the way in which the GATS may help Union non-member countries to reduce competitive disadvantages created among other things by discriminatory measures against outsiders, and where loopholes exist (Gugler 1993a).[57]

Following Hoekman and Sauvé (1993), six criteria may be used in order to compare Union and the GATS: 1) the modalities and instruments that are used to liberalize services markets, 2) sectoral coverage; 3) disciplines with regards to government practices in areas such as subsidies and public procurement; 4) enforcement and dispute settlement procedures; 5) rules of origin and 6) safeguard provisions. These six criteria may help to determine the significance of Union liberalization and thus the impact on both Member States and outsiders (Table 34).

The program of the Single European Act aims at a degree of liberalization of services markets whose scope goes beyond what may emerge in the GATS. For example:

- The Union forms a common labor market that is not reproduced in the GATS, which covers only the temporary movement of natural persons supplying services.
- The GATS encourages the negotiation of recognition agreements without imposing any obligation, whereas the Union mandates the harmonization or mutual recognition of regulatory regimes pertaining to licensing and certification in some sectors.[58]

---

[57] Treaties other than GATS may also contribute to circumventing EC 1992 effects on outsiders, such as the OECD codes for Capital Movement and for Invisible Operations, membership in the Union, bilateral agreements with the Union (such as in the Swiss case, road transport transit agreement and insurance agreement) and multilateral agreements with the EC such as the EEA Treaty (Nunnenkamp, 1993; Lautenberg, 1992). For example, Switzerland and the Union have concluded agreements on non-life insurance and on road transport transit.

[58] Non-Union states may be reluctant to conclude mutual negotiation agreements with the Union in areas where the Union policy is liberal because these states do not want to implement liberalized rules in their legislation. In this way, some countries may discriminate against themselves.

Table 33. Modes of supply.

SUPPLIER PRESENCE	OTHER CRITERIA	MODE
Services supplier not present within the territory of the Member	Service delivered within the territory of the Member, from from territory of another Member	CROSS-BORDER SUPPLY
	Service delivered outside the territory of the Member, in the territory of another Member, to a service consumer of the Member	CONSUMPTION ABROAD
Service supplier present within the territory of the Member	Service delivered within the territory of the Member, through the commercial presence of the supplier	COMMERCIAL PRESENCE
	Service delivered within the territory of the Member, with supplier present as a natural person	PRESENCE OF NATURAL PERSON

Source: GATT Secretariat, Informal note on scheduling guidelines, 20 June 1993.
Member = Member of GATS

- The GATS allows for MFN derogation whereas Union does not.
- Commitments on market access and national treatment in GATS are only related to scheduled sectors.
- Public procurements: no specific rules are settled in GATS (except provisions of Article XIII), while the Union liberalizes public procurements.

This comparison indicates that the EC92 program involves a degree of liberalization that is unlikely to be matched by GATS in the near future. The major gap between the GATS and the EC92 program seems to be in the abolition of non-trade barriers by mutual recognition and harmonization procedures.

To assess more precisely the role of the GATS for outsiders to EC92, three items have to be examined: the Union schedule of commitments with regard to market access and national treatment; the relationship

Table 34. Comparison of EC-92 program and the GATS.

Agreement criteria	EC-1992	GATS
1) Modalities and instruments of liberalization	• Four freedoms: goods, services, capital, labor • Nondiscrimination: all modes of supply liberalized. No exemptions to general nondiscrimination requirements • Implicit right of non-establishment. Harmonization of prudential and safety regulations • Common labor market • Mutual recognition of diplomas and certification of professional service providers • Accession negotiations	All modes of supply covered in principle. Transparency, MFN, and dispute settlement as a core general obligations. National treatment and market access for scheduled sectors only. No general right of non-establishment. Encouragement of recognition agreements for licensing and certification requirements. No general disciplines on non-discriminatory quantitative restrictions, but these prohibited under the market access article unless explicitly reserved
2) Sectoral coverage	• All services covered • Sector-specific directives • Common EC policy for transport	Positive list of scheduled sectors. Most air transport services excluded via an annex (indefinite). Other annexes deal with telecommunications (access to and use of public networks and services); financial services (complemented by an Understanding of commitments on financial services); movement of natural persons. Content of country schedules currently under negotiation.
3) Disciplines on related government policies	• Government procurement services, including construction, covered • State aid subject to restrictions and monitoring	No disciplines for government procurement. MFN obligation for subsidies. Subsidy disciplines to be negotiated in future. Services and construction procurement under discussion in context of GATT Code on government procurement.
4) Enforcement and dispute settlement	• EC law has direct effect; supersedes national laws • Enforcement by private parties and the European commission • Supranational court of Justice • No service-specific procedures	General procedures under the MTO (multilateral trade organization). Consultations followed by a panel. Strict time limits imposed for the various stages of the dispute settlement process. Non-implementation of panel findings may result in authorization of retaliatory measures.
5) Rules of origin	Incorporation in an EC Member State and headquarters or principal place of business in the EC	Nationality or residency for natural persons; incorporation under the laws of a Party and substantive business operations in a Party; or control - ownership by nationals of a Party. Ownership requires the power to direct the actions of the enterprise.
6) Safeguards	Only one service-specific provision relating to the common transport policy. General balance of payments and public health and safety provisions	Provides for services specific measures to safeguard the balance of payments and to protect service industries injured by import competition. However, specific rules on the latter to be negotiated. Also provides for modification of commitments, subject to compensation of affected Parties.

Source: Adapted from: Hoeckman and Sauvé, 1993, pp. 64-67.

between GATS and the EC92 regarding the discrimination by the Union of third countries *vis-à-vis* Member States; and the relationship between GATS and the EC92 regarding the discrimination by the Union of third countries *vis-à-vis* third countries (for example, preferential treatment accorded by the Union to the United States but not to Japan).

The Union Schedule of commitments

As mentioned above, each member has to make commitments listed in a national schedule. This schedule represents the level of liberalization to which the country in question has bound itself.

The Union makes commitments in major service sectors, such as: professional services, telecommunication services, distribution services, construction services, privately funded education services, environmental services, financial services (banking, insurance), health services and social services, tourism and travel-related services and transport services.

As far as labor mobility is concerned, the Union makes commitments for the temporary presence of key personnel (intracorporate transferees and representatives of a service provider not established in the Union). However, the limited developments under the GATS on matters relating to labor mobility, combined with the maintenance of discriminatory immigration and residency requirements, do not lead to the withdrawal of certain discriminatory practices, particularly in the professional service sectors.

The sectors and subsectors listed in the European Union's schedule, such as architectural and engineering services, are not necessarily offered without restrictions (residency restrictions, economic needs tests, etc.). Also, the Union does not take on any commitments in some subsectors such as:

- audiovisual services
- basic telecommunications[59]
- passenger and freight air transportation (according to the annex on air transport these activities are excluded from the GATS)

---

[59] However, commitments with regards to basic telecommunications could be made in the context of the negotiations on basic telecommunications which should be finished in April 1996.

Discriminatory measures –
Union members vis-à-vis non-members

Regional agreements (such as the Union) are, by definition, discriminatory. However, GATS (Articles XXIV and V) allow regional arrangements under certain conditions.[60] As far as services are concerned, Article V (GATS) allows economic integration arrangements, provided that such agreements:

- Have substantial sectoral coverage (in terms of number of sectors, volume of trade affected and modes of supply). In order to meet this condition, it is stated that agreements should not provide for the *a priori* exclusion of any mode of supply.
- Provide for the absence or elimination of substantially all discrimination (in the sense of the provisions of Article XVII on national treatment) between or among the parties, in the sectors covered by the agreement, through elimination of existing discriminatory measures and/or prohibition of new or additional discriminatory measures.

Thus, according to Article V (GATS), the Union Member States may accord among themselves a preferential treatment that does not have to be granted on an MFN basis to the other GATS members.

As noted earlier, the EC92 program goes beyond the GATS in terms of the scope and extent of the liberalization measures. For example, the harmonization and mutual recognition program of the Union – which plays a crucial role in the service sector – is not reproduced in GATS. According to a reservation specified in the Union schedule on commitments, Union directives on mutual recognition of diplomas do not apply to nationals of third countries. Recognition of diplomas required in order to practice regulated professional activities by non Union nationals remains within the competence of each Member State (unless provided otherwise by Union law), and the right to practice in one Member State does not grant the right to practice in another member State.

However, according to Article VII (GATS), a party to a recognition agreement or arrangement, whether future or existing, shall afford adequate opportunity for other interested members to negotiate their accession to such agreements or arrangements or to negotiate comparable ones

---

[60] For a discussion on Article XXIV of GATTs, see Hoekman and Leidy (1992, pp. 325-360).

with it. Where a member accords recognition autonomously, it shall afford adequate opportunity for other members to demonstrate that education, experience, licenses, or certifications obtained or requirements met in their territories should be recognized. As recognition of the education or experience, requirements, or licenses or certifications is very important in the liberalization of trade in many service sectors and subsectors (such as professional services), Article VII provides for some measures towards developing an extension of intra-Union recognition to non-members.

To assess the importance of the potential of discrimination by the Union between non-Member States' service providers and those in Union Member States, we have to compare the difference between the level of liberalization achieved within the Union and the level of liberalization offered in the Union national schedule. The comparison between the Union regime of liberalization inside the Union and the Union schedule in the GATS (for outsiders to the Union) is very complex and goes beyond the objectives of this study. However, in general, the main differences may be seen as follows.

Major discrimination specific to a particular sector

- *Telecommunications.*

  The Union program on liberalization of telecommunication is based on several directives (for example, Council Directive of 5 June 1992 on the application of the open network provision to leased lines; Council Directive of 28 June 1990 on the establishment of the internal market for telecommunications services through the implementation of the open network provision; and Commission Directive of 28 June 1990 on competition in markets for telecommunications services). The process of liberalization is under way and the objective of the Union is full liberalization of all telecommunication services by 1998. However, concerning basic telecommunication services, the Union is not yet fully liberalized, though new proposals to liberalize basic telecommunications are under way. As far as enhanced telecommunication services (value added services) are concerned, the Union policy *vis-à-vis* non-members is quite open: the Union has taken on commitments on the main value-added services without any restrictions. Thus the discrimination is not yet significant, but the risk of a major discrepancy between members and non-members is real, because the Union offer does not cover basic telecommunications. The process of liberalization in the Union goes further than in GATS, whose annex applies only to measures that affect access to and the use of public telecommunications transport networks and services. But, according to the future multilateral negotiation on liberalization of basic telecommunications under the auspices of GATS (which will take place from April 1994 until April 1996), the risks of discrimination faced by non-members could be reduced.

- *Financial services.*

  Besides the reciprocity regime – mentioned below – discrimination may appear with regard to cross-border trade (for example, a German insurance company may sell insurance to a resident in France without being established in France, whereas a Japanese insurance company is not allowed to do the same). Another example: the Economic and Monetary Union will lead to the abolition of exchange-rate operations and of exchange risks in the Union, which will yield cost advantages to Union-established firms for Union-internal transactions (Blankart 1991).

- *Audiovisual.*

  Discrimination measures may result from the subsidization foreseen in promotion programs of the Union and other European institutions, and from quotas in some States.

- *Air transportation.*

  Discrimination against non-member carriers within the Union regarding the transportation of passengers and freight, for example, cabotage (now in the process of intra-Union liberalization). Air fare freedom is not allowed for non-Union carriers within the Union.

- *Professional services.*

  Obstacles linked to diplomas, experience and residency requirements in some Member States.

Discrimination related to public procurement

In the field of public procurement, Article XIII (GATS) states that Articles II (MFN), XVI (market access) and XVII (national treatment) shall not apply to rules governing the procurement by governmental agencies of services purchased for governmental purposes. However, Article XIII states also that there shall be multilateral negotiations on government procurements in services under the GATS within two years from the entry into force of the agreement. For the time being, discrimination in the field of public procurement is not preventable by GATT

In the Union, national procurement entities are required to apply Union rules to all supplies of goods and services worth more than ECU 200,000. However, in the formerly "excluded sectors" (water, energy, transport and telecommunications), a new Union directive (93/38) sets the amount at ECU 400,000 or in telecommunications at 60,000. In these sectors the directive permits the rejection of offers with a foreign content of over 50% from countries that do not grant equivalent access to Union supplies and requires Union preferences to be given if the price differential is 3% or less. However, these discriminations may be avoided according to the provisions of Article 36 of the Directive, which states that third countries that do grant equivalent access to Union suppliers won't be discriminated any more in the Union.

At the multilateral level, the new GATS Agreement on Government Procurement establishes a framework of rights and obligations with respect to regulations, laws, procedures and practices concerning public procurements.[61] However, this agreement (for example, the MFN discipline), adopted by thirteen parties such as the Union, the United States, Japan, Canada, Switzerland and Israel, does partly regulate government procurement at the local level. Public procurement with regard to private entities operating in the field of the services governed by Directive 93/38 is completely excluded.

Bilateral agreements with the Union – under the auspices of the GATT Agreement on Government Procurement – may provide for the avoidance of discrimination, on a reciprocal basis, in the "excluded sectors". In the Swiss case, bilateral agreements with the Union have already been concluded in the fields of water, energy and transport (excluding railways). Discussions leading toward the achievement of an agreement in the field of railways and telecommunications are underway.

Discriminatory measures – the unequal status of Union non-members

Discriminatory measures, non-members/non-members, may also be allowed according to Article V (GATS) for all economic integration agreements concluded by the Union and other non-member countries, under the condition that these agreements fall under Article V provisions. The EEA agreement between the Union and the EFTA countries (except Switzerland) is one example.

---

[61] The new Agreement on Government Procurement will come into force on 1 January 1996. This new Agreement improves and expands the scope of the current Agreement on Government Procurement, which is an amended version of the Agreement of 1979 resulting from the Tokyo Round.

As indicated above, Article II (GATS), paragraph 1, states that each member shall accord treatment immediately and unconditionally to services and service providers of any other member, treatment no less favorable than that it accords to like services and service providers of any other country. However according to paragraph 2 of Article II, a member may maintain a measure inconsistent with MFN principles under some conditions specified in an annex. According to this annex, each member may submit an MFN exemption list – to be negotiated with the other members – which allows it to apply discriminatory measures, such as reciprocity clauses, preferential treatment, etc.[62] The Union has submitted a MFN exemption list that covers *inter alia* the following sectors: audiovisual, internal waterway transport, maritime transport and road transport.

As indicated above, countries may conclude bilateral agreements with the Union in specific areas in order to promote and facilitate trade between the two parties. However, due to Article II (GATS) on MFN principles, conclusion of bilateral agreements may be more difficult to achieve in the future. Indeed, the Union may be more reluctant to accord preferential treatment to another country through a bilateral agreement because, according to Article II, this preferential treatment (originally accorded to one country) has to be extended to all GATS parties, unless an MFN derogation has been requested in order to prevent this extension.

Reciprocity may constitute a discriminatory threat to outsiders. However, as indicated in the Preamble of Directives dealing with reciprocity, "the purpose of the reciprocity clause (...) is not to create a 'Fortress Europe' within which EC institutions would be sheltered from international competition but, rather, to promote liberalization by non-EC country and thereby increase the competitive opportunities for EC institutions in third country markets" (OECD 1990). The second banking directive (Second Council Directive of 15 December 1989 on the coordination of laws, regulations and administrative provisions relating to the taking up and pursuit of the business of credit instituions and amending Directive 77/780/EEC) introduces the concept of Union-wide reciprocity in the banking field. In this respect, reciprocity may be used by the Union in the banking sector as a tool for protection and retaliation, and also as a tool of

---

[62] However, a Member that takes a national treatment and/or a market access commitment in a sector must accord the stated minimum standard of treatment specified in its schedule to all other Members. Where an MFN exemption has been granted, a Member is free to deviate from its Art. II obligations, but not from its Article XVI and XVII commitments.

market liberalization. Indeed, Union third country banks may operate throughout the Union under a single license only if Union banks are allowed to do the same in the third countries. However, at this stage, the Union has not submitted a MFN exemption for reciprocity in the banking sector. That means that reciprocity may be invoked as a bargaining chip in the negotiation process.

V. Conclusions

The completion of the European internal market constitutes a major challenge in Europe as well as in other parts of the world, particularly for the main trading partners of the Union Member States. The changes induced by the European internal market are particularly important in service sectors, whose liberalization within the Union was quite slow – compared with the goods sector – until 1985. More concretely, the completion of the EC92 program, followed by the enlargement of the Union, affects the comparative advantages of third countries and the competitive advantages of their enterprises. In order to successfully face these challenges, adequate responses by the firms as well as by the countries themselves are necessary. As far as firms' strategies are concerned, it has been shown in this chapter that Swiss firms have increased their FDI within the Union and their strategic alliances with the European Union's partners. Concerning the policy responses, several options are possible for third countries in order to respond to a regional integration agreement. The main options are: (a) to strengthen the multilateral trading system; (b) to join the regional integration agreement; or (c) to conclude bilateral agreements with the regional integration agreement. As far as the last two options are concerned, in the Swiss case, the (c) option prevails since the (b) option seems to be politically impossible in the near future. However, whereas the (c) option may only reduce some discriminatory measures and enhance security of market access in a limited number of sectors, the (a) option is of crucial importance.

Thus, the objective of this chapter has been to examine to what extent the GATS reduces Union discriminatory practices applied to the European Union's non-members' firms, particularly in the case of Swiss firms, in the context of the EC92 program in services. It has been shown that the EC92 program on services goes beyond the GATS in terms of scope and obligations, leading to a liberalization of trade in services. However, the

GATS constitutes an important agreement that gives the legal insurance to third countries – such as Switzerland – that they will benefit from a given stage of liberalization (stated by the general obligations and the Union schedule on initial commitments). Nevertheless, the GATS leaves some "holes and loopholes" that could decrease in the future due to the progressive liberalization principle foreseen by the GATS.

However, these "holes and loopholes" create new challenges for the Swiss firms as well as for the Swiss government. This situation constitutes a typical case illustrating the way in which the competitive advantages of firms both affect and are affected by the comparative advantages of countries and how each of them influences the ways in which resources and capabilities are organized across national markets (Dunning and Narula 1993c). Therefore, the current domestic policy responses and new corporate strategies of Swiss firms, interacting with each other, are necessary to pursue in order to counteract these disadvantages.

Appendix

General Agreement on rade in Services (GATS)

Preamble

Part I   **Scope and Definition**
            Article I   Scope and Definition

Part II   **General Obligations and Disciplines**
            Article II   Most-Favoured-Nation Treatment
            Article III   Transparency
            Article II bis   Disclosure of Confidential Information
            Article IV   Increasing Participation of Developing Countries
            Article V   Economic Integration
            Article VI   Domestic Regulation
            Article VII   Restrictions to Safeguard the Balance of Payments
            Article VIII   Monopolies and Exclusive Service Providers
            Article IX   Business Practices
            Article X   Emergency Safeguard Measures
            Article XI   Payments and Transfers
            Article XII   Restrictions to Safeguard the Balance of Payments
            Article XIII   Government Procurement
            Article XIV   General Exceptions
            Article XIV bis   Security Exceptions
            Article XV   Subsidies

Part III   **Specific Commitments**
            Article XVI   Market Access
            Article XVII   National Treatment
            Article XVIII   Additional Commitments

Part IV   **Progressive Liberalization**
            Article XIX   Negotiation of Commitments
            Article XX   Schedules of Commitments
            Article XXI   Modification of Schedules

Part V   **Institutional Provisions**
            Article XXII   Consultation
            Article XXIII   Dispute Settlement and Enforcement
            Article XXIV   Council for Trade in Services
            Article XXV   Technical Cooperation
            Article XXVI   Relationship with other International Organizations

Part VI   **Final Provisions**
            Article XXVII   Denial of Benefits
            Article XXVIII   Definitions
            Article XXXIX   Annexes

Annexes:
            Annex on Article II Exemptions
            Annex on Movement of Natural Persons Providing
            Services under the Agreement
            Annex on Financial Services
            Annex on Telecommunications Services
            Annex on Basic Telecommunications Services
            Annex on Maritime Transport Services
            Annex on Air Transport Services

Source: GATT Secretariat, 1993.

References

Bhagwati, J. (1992): *Regionalism and Multilateralism: An Overview.* Discussion Paper Series. New York: Columbia University.

Blankart, F. (1991): *The Maastricht Summit and its impact upon the EEA.* Geneva: Graduate Institute for International Studies. Unpublished)

Braunerhjelm, P. and L. Oxelheim (1993): *Heckscher-Ohlin and Schumpeter Industries: The Response by Swedish Multinational Firms to the EC 1992 Program.* Copenhagen: Institute of International Economics and Management, WP 5-93.

Carlisle, C. R. (1991): *Remarks on the Uruguay Round Negotiations. The Geneva Papers on Risk and Insurance Issues and Practice,* No.61. Geneva: Geneva Association: 401-404.

Dunning J. H. (1988): Cross-border Corporate Integration and Regional Integration. In J. H. Dunning (ed.) *Explaining International Trade.* London: Unwin Hyman: 291-305.

Dunning, J. H. (1993a): *The Globalization of Business.* London: Routledge.

Dunning, J. H. (1993b): *Globalization: the Challenge for National Economic Regimes.* Presented at the Symposium on Globalisation, OECD.

Dunning, J. H. and R. Narula (1993c): *Transpacific Foreign Direct Investment and the Investment Development Path: the Record Assessed.* Maastricht: MERIT.

Fieleke, N. S. (1992): One Trading World or Many: The Issue of Regional Trading Blocs, *New England Economic Review,* 1-20.

GATT Secretariat (1993): *Final Act Embodying the Results of the Uruguay Round of Multilateral Trade Negotiations.* MTN/FA, 13 December 1993.

GATT Secretariat (1993b): *Informal Note on Scheduling Guidelines,* 20 July 1993.

Gaudard G. (1989): L'ouverture du marché des services. *Revue économique et sociale,* no 4. Lausanne: 205-213.

Gugler P., (1992): Building Transnational Alliances to Create Competive Advantages, Long Range Planning, Vol. 25, No. 1, pp. 90-99.

Gugler, P. and J. H. Dunning (1994): Technology Based Cross-border Alliances. In D. J. Jeremy (ed.) *Technology Transfer and Business Enterprise.* Brookfield: Edward Elgar Publishing Company.

Gugler, P. (1993b): *General Agreement on Trade in Services (GATS): An Outsider response to EC-1992 in Trade in Services?* Working Paper No. 226. Fribourg: Centre of Research in Spatial Economics of the University of Fribourg, Institute For Economic and Social Sciences, University of Fribourg.

Hirsch S. and T. Almor (1992): *Outsiders' Response to Europe 1992: Theoretical Considerations and Empirical Evidence.* Copenhagen: Institute of International Economics and Management. Working Paper No. 9-92.

Hoekman, B. (1992): International Cooperation on Measures Affecting Trade in Services. Geneva: UNCTC-World Bank.

Hoekman, B. and M. P. Leidy (1992): Holes and Loopholes in Regional Trade Arrangements and the Multilateral Trading System. *Aussenwirtschaft,* Volume 47: 325-360.

Hoekman, B. and P. Sauvé (1993): *Regional and Multilateral Liberalization of Services Markets: Complements or Substitutes.* Internal Paper on GATT. Unpublished.

Kern, S. (1994): *Eine empirische Studie über strategische Allianzen von Schweizer Unternehmungen.* Berne: University of Berne.

Kuznets, S. (1960): Economic growth of small nations. In E.A.G. Robinson (ed.) *Economic Consequences of the Size of Nations.* New York: St. Martin's Press: 14-32.

Lautenberg, A.P. (1992): *Globale und Regionale Liberalisierung der Bank und Finanzdienstleistungen.* 3. Internationaler Kongree für europäische Finanz und Wirtschaftsentwicklungstendenzen, Gstaad.

Lawson, D. (1992): *A Study of Regional Economic Development Theory and Marketing Strategy in a Developed Country Context.* Presented at the DSRI, Gilleleje, Denmark.

Loyd, P. J. (1992): Regionalisation and World Trade. *OECD Economic Studies 18*: 7-43.

Nunnenkamp, P. (1993): The World Trading System at the Crossroads: Multilateral Trade Negotiations in the Era of Regionalism. *Aussenwirtschaft,* Volume 48: 177-201.

OECD (1990): *EC Directive on Credit Institutions.* Paris: OECD.

OECD (1994): *Etudes économiques de l'OCDE: Suisse.* Paris: OECD.

Ruane, F. (1990): *Internationalization of Services: Conceptual and Empirical Issues,* Dublin: Trinity College.

Scitovsky, T. (1960): International trade and economic integration as a means of overcoming the disadvantages of a small nation. In E. A. G. Robinson (ed.): *Economic Consequences of the Size of Nations.* New York: St. Martins Press: 14-32.

Zweifel P. (ed.) (1993): *Services in Switzerland: Structure, Performance and Implication of European Economic Integration. Berlin:* Springer Verlag.

Chapter 7:
Responding to Unification of the European Community
The Use of International Strategic Alliances by Outsiders

Tamar Almor

Creation of a single European market is purported to bring about a host of changes. Studies pertaining to changes in specific industries as well as reports regarding the overall effect of creation of the single market have been published by the European Union (Cecchini 1988). It is clear that the changes in the Union environment are pervasive enough to create a situation in which firms rethink their strategic position and adapt their strategy accordingly. It is further important to realize that the changes in the Union environment not only affect insider (Union) firms but outsider firms as well. Much research has been published regarding the response of insider as well as outsider firms to the changes taking place in the Union environment (Buigues and Jacquemin 1989; Burgemeier and Mucchielli 1991; Denis and Burke 1989; Dunning 1991; Franko 1989; Rugman and Verbeke 1991). However, most of this research has focused on foreign direct investment (FDI) strategies. For instance the European Commission reported that FDI by third countries increased from ECU 14,919 million in 1980 to ECU 39,674 million in 1988 (Monthly Newsletter 1990). Similarly, such researchers as Ozawa (1992) and Rugman and Verbeke (1991) have used FDI data to study responses to creation of a single European market, also called Europe 1992 (EC92).

In this chapter we focus on another type of response strategy, namely international strategic alliances. International strategic alliances have gained attention during the last years as a popular strategy that is chosen by small as well as large firms to compete outside their home country. The Seventeenth Report on Competition Policy (Commission of the European Communities 1988) shows that outsider firms not only increased FDI in the Union but also employed international strategic alliances more frequently. International strategic alliances enable firms to establish a foothold in the Union while exploiting the advantages of a partnership with an insider firm, thus becoming insiders. In other words, international strategic alliances present outsider firms with an alternative response to the changes taking place in the Union environment.

This chapter looks at international strategic alliances in relation to environmental change created by EC92. Strategists argue that the environment presents the firm with a given situation that is analyzed in terms of opportunities and threats, matched to the firm's strengths and weaknesses and subsequently acted upon. In this chapter it is argued that 1) although strategic alliances can take different forms they are variations upon one archetype strategy and 2) this archetype is used as a response strategy that is employed by firms experiencing environmental change.

The analysis is based on data gathered at the level of the firm. All participants in the study were Israeli manufacturers that marketed their products in the Union prior to 1993.

Different paradigms have been offered as to why firms prefer international strategic alliances over other types of international strategy. In the first part of this chapter a theoretical framework is presented, discussing various theories on strategic alliances and their relation to environmental change. Subsequently the changing Union environment is analyzed. In the last part of this chapter, empirical data are presented that show the occurrence of Israeli international strategic alliances in the Union. It also shows the various objectives obtained through the international strategic alliance by the firms in the sample and the use of international strategic alliances by firms in various industries.

I. International Strategic Alliances

Firms operating in the international business environment frequently choose international strategies that are more sophisticated than export of products and/or services. Various explanations have been offered as to why firms choose such sophisticated international strategies (Aharoni 1966; Dunning 1988; Franko 1987; Jarillo 1988; Porter 1990). The choice of international strategy seems to depend, among others, on the degree of change in the environment in which the international firm operates (Ghemawat, Porter and Rawlinson 1986; Porter and Fuller 1986). The use of international strategic alliances is one type of international strategy employed by firms operating in changing international environments.

Theories of strategic alliances do not distinguish between national and international alliances as such. International strategic alliances are perceived to be a viable option for firms that operate in global markets (Franko 1987; Ghemawat, Porter and Fuller 1986; Hamel, Doz and Prahalad 1988; Negandi and Donhowe 1989; Ohmae 1989; Porter and Fuller 1986). Firms that operate internationally face a complex, uncertain world, in which change is the only constant (Negandi and Donhowe 1989), in which it is best not to go it alone (Ohmae 1989). Firms therefore have to be willing to adopt new and more flexible strategies such as strategic alliances.

International strategic alliances do not necessarily involve foreign investment. They are characterized by the fact that tangible as well as intangible assets are pooled in order to achieve a specific objective. When tangible assets are involved, the alliance may represent a specific case of FDI. However, they do not necessarily depend on investments in tangible or financial assets.

A number of rationales have been offered as to why firms seek strategic alliances, including the theories of strategic behavior, resource dependence and transaction costs.

Strategic alliances are based on the presumption that each partner has something the other wants or needs. From the strategic behavior point of view, the alliance enables a firm to achieve a strategic objective that may be otherwise unattainable (Harrigan 1988; Porter and Fuller 1986). Following this reasoning, a wide range of motives can cause firms to seek strategic alliances. For instance, firms may seek to exchange or pool resources in order to achieve economy of scale. They may seek to exchange or pool technologies, production processes, knowledge of markets, or R&D functions, in order to achieve a competitive advantage over competitors, to enter markets, or to gain access to technologies or production processes that have high entrance barriers. In essence, the strategic behavior school views strategic alliances as an option to enlarge the firm's ability to cope with opportunities and threats in the environment.

Both resource dependence (Pfeffer and Salancik 1978) and the transaction costs theory (Balakrishnan and Koza 1988; Jarillo 1988; Thorelli 1986) are based on the assumption that a firm will only use alliances if internalization of resources, that is, acquisition or merging, is not possible or less efficient. However, the two theories differ in their explanation of the context in which alliances are sought.

Resource dependence has been employed by a number of researchers in their explanation of the occurrence of alliances (Contractor and Lorange 1988; Pennings 1981; Pfeffer and Nowak 1976; Pfeffer and Salancik 1978). Pfeffer and Nowak (1976) argue that firms face two types of organizational interdependence: competitive and symbiotic interdependence. Competitive interdependence occurs when firms compete with similar products and services for the same markets, while symbiotic interdependence occurs when firms are mutually dependent upon each other in the value added chain. Both types of interdependence are created when:

> "one actor does not entirely control all the conditions necessary
> for the achievement of an action or for obtaining the outcome
> desired from the action" (Pfeffer and Salancik 1978:40).

Consequently, interdependence creates uncertainty for firms, which they want to minimize. One way of controlling interdependence is by absorbing the elements that create the most uncertainty, that is, on which the firm is most critically dependent. However, when absorption is not possible, firms may opt to seek interorganizational cooperation in the form of alliances.

The transaction costs theory is derived from Williamson's (1975) concept of markets and hierarchies as two alternative modes of organizing economic activities. Williamson (1975) argued that firms seek the most efficient way to access needed resources. When no transaction costs are involved, the firm will purchase the needed resources through a spot transaction or on an arm's-length basis. However, if transaction costs such as opportunism, early mover advantages, and other uncertain elements are involved, a firm will prefer to integrate the needed functions into its hierarchy. A third alternative to gain access to needed resources is through strategic alliances (Balakrishnan and Koza 1989). Strategic alliances are preferable when the cost of valuing needed resources is non-trivial and piecemeal transactions under shared ownership and control are called for.

Besides these theoretical approaches, a number of context specific explanations for the occurrence of international strategic alliances have been offered. These are based on the assumption that environmental change and unpredictability trigger the use of international strategic alliances. For instance, researchers (Hergert and Morris 1988; Porter and Fuller 1986; Pucik 1988) argue that firms that operate in an unpredictable environment where the variance of return is very large, as in the development of new technologies, will prefer to share the risk rather than go it alone. Powell (1987) argues that when the environment is very dynamic, firms will prefer alliances as a way to reposition themselves quickly without incurring the high costs associated with internalization and without loss of flexibility. Summarizing, it is clear that the environmental context, either in terms of uncertainty or change, plays an important role in the explanation of the existence of strategic alliances.

Strategic alliances have been characterized in various ways, for example, on the basis of strategic motives (Mariti and Smiley 1983), strategic function (Kogut 1988), legal contract (Contractor and Lorange 1988) and partner symmetries/asymmetries (Harrigan 1988). International strategic alliances often take the form of international joint ventures, equity partnerships, technology swaps, joint R&D, reciprocity deals or joint production. In this chapter the following general definition of international strategic alliances is proposed:

> *Contractual agreements that exist for a certain purpose and period of time, set up between firms based in different countries, linking aspects of their business in such a way that mutual dependence is created.*[63]

This definition implicitly assumes that all international strategic alliances belong to the same generic strategy, which is situated in between spot transactions and internalization strategies. It also implies that the form of international strategic alliance chosen by the partners will be situation dependent and not necessarily have explanatory value. Indeed, Porter and Fuller (1986) as well as Powell (1987) argued that the form of the alliance is mainly a function of local tax and regulatory considerations and does not say much about the purpose of the cooperation.

Based on the literature review presented above, it is argued in this study that firms use international strategic alliances in foreign markets when a) they perceive (unpredictable) changes in that environment and b) they interpret new opportunities and threats that they cannot exploit by themselves alone.

---

[63] Not included are mergers, acquisitions or wholly owned subsidiaries.

II. Environmental Change:
Creation of a Single European Market

Creation of a single European market is the result of a plan set out originally in 1957 in the EEC treaty to create a common market. The process
of Europe 1992 has become more tangible since June 1985, when the
Commission of the European Communities issued a White Paper called
Completing the Internal Market. This paper discusses 282 proposals and
measures (directives) that, taken together, are geared to enable the Community to achieve a single European market for goods, services, people,
capital and (the harmonization of) taxes by January 1, 1993. Most of the
directives were in various stages of implementation before the target date,
some will be implemented later. As a result, extensive changes are taking
place in the Union environment. Because the process is an ongoing one,
quite a measure of uncertainty still exists regarding the future market and
industry structures and the positioning of competitors.

The disappearance of traditional market boundaries, such as national
borders, combined with the lowering of certain trade barriers as well as the
expected growth in consumer demand, are perceived by many firms as an
opportunity to grow and expand their markets in the Union (Cecchini
1988). However, growth in consumer demand as well as altered market
segmentation may not be sufficient to enable expansion by all firms simultaneously. As a result, intensified competition is expected between firms
already operating in the Union, while competition is enhanced even more
by new competitors interested in exploiting the same opportunities (Baldwin 1989; Daems 1990). Large companies will be able to exploit the
enlarged markets and diminished barriers for previously unrealized economies of scale in R&D, production processes and marketing. Many small
and medium-sized enterprises will find it increasingly difficult to compete
in the enlarged markets alone, as most do not have the required resources to compete on such a scale. On the other hand, new niches will be
created that, because of their size, are not attractive to large firms and will
appeal mainly to small and medium-sized enterprises employing focus
strategies. Thus the unification process is creating changes in the Union
business environment that pose a measure of uncertainty, changes that can
be interpreted as presenting opportunities for some companies and posing
threats to others.

EC92 is an internal process not intended to affect the relationships
between the Union and outsiders. Therefore, one could maintain that, if
trade barriers facing outsiders that operate in the Union market are not

going to be affected, outsiders should not be concerned with change. This may be a shortsighted argument, since the relative competitive position of the outside competitor in the Union market will change as a result of EC92. By changing the competitive position of insiders, EC92 will have a profound effect on all competitors, whether insiders or outsiders (Hirsch 1989; Almor and Hirsch 1995; Ohlsson 1989). Union-based firms will face increased competition in their home markets as a result of the unification process, as diminished barriers previously protecting home markets attract new competition from other Member States. However, while the competitive position of the Union firm in its home market is threatened, new opportunities are created for that same firm in other Member State markets. The same firms, which previously operated in a foreign market when penetrating the markets of other European countries, can now consider these same markets to be a home market and will be able to expand into these markets as if they were in their own national markets. This differs from the position of outsider firms, still faced with a having to cross at least one border to enter the Union market. Hence, the outsider firm will continue to operate in a foreign (Union) market, while the position of its Union competitor has improved. (For an extensive discussion, see Almor and Hirsch 1995.) The competitive position of outsiders will deteriorate even further: they will not be able to participate in government procurement tenders, nor is it clear whether or what type of mutual recognition for product standards will exist between the Union and third countries.

From the above discussion it follows that both insider and outsider firms are operating in a changing environment. The degrees of change may differ among industries as well as individual firms. Nonetheless, all firms in that specific environment will have to face some change. The occurrence of objective change however, does not necessarily warrant strategic action. Strategic action, or a response to change, will depend upon the perception and interpretation of change. Thus, after change is perceived and data are gathered, it needs to be interpreted in terms of opportunities and threats. While some changes will be perceived as posing an opportunity for the firm (for example, enlargement of markets) others may be viewed as threats (for example, more competitors). Depending on the interpretation of the change, firms will decide how to respond and what type of strategic action to take. It should be kept in mind that a response to change does not imply reactive (as opposed to proactive) behavior (Miles and Snow 1978). Indeed, timely perception of a change in the environment is part of proactive behavior.

As was shown in the first chapter of this book, interpretation of change is mediated by the type of industry. Almor and Hirsch (1995) argue that firms that manufacture products containing a significant element of proprietary knowledge – knowledge that imparts unique characteristics to the product and that can be effectively withheld from competitors – will be affected differently than firms that produce products based on universal knowledge. The Schumpeter goods, products based on proprietary knowledge, are associated with services that depend on firm-specific knowledge. A firm producing Schumpeter goods that are sold in a foreign market will need to stay involved in that market, either directly or through agents, in order to service its products over time. Firms producing universal or Heckscher-Ohlin goods, on the other hand, do not depend on the possession of proprietary knowledge. The technology is easily acquired and does not confer a competitive advantage on the firm that possesses it. Therefore Heckscher-Ohlin firms can unbundle their value chain since the knowledge required to service the products is in the public domain. Thus the products can be serviced by any independent actor.

EC92 presents new opportunities for Schumpeter goods manufacturers. As Schumpeter goods manufacturers have to be more involved in their target market than Heckscher-Ohlin goods manufacturers, it makes sense to invest in forward integration, especially when the market is relatively large. Until January 1, 1993, the Union was a fragmented market that did not encourage cross-border provision of services, thus forcing Schumpeter goods manufacturers to duplicate their service outlets or to operate through independent service providers. Creation of a single European market enables Schumpeter goods manufacturers to provide services across borders to any client located in one of the Member States. This change provides Member States' Schumpeter goods manufacturers with the opportunity to consolidate service facilities. The change further encourages insider firms that could not afford or were not interested in duplication of their service stations to service clients all over the Union from their manufacturing plant.

Schumpeter goods manufacturers situated in third countries (outsiders) will have to set up a local presence in order to exploit the same opportunities in the Union market. Indeed, data presented in previous chapters show that the propensity of outsider Schumpeter goods manufacturers to invest in the Union is higher than that of Heckscher-Ohlin goods manufacturers, especially in light of the unification of the Union.

III. Outsider Response to Unification of the European Community: The Case of Israel

The discussion in the preceding sections suggests that international strategic alliances are likely to figure prominently among the strategies employed by outsiders to cope with the changes in the Union environment, in order to counteract the negative and exploit the positive aspects of this change. International strategic alliances are likely to be particularly important for international firms originating from small economies that trade intensively with the European Union. Israel is such an economy.

Israel is a small country with an open economy, highly dependent on international transactions for its economic well being. Exports plus imports reached 83% of its GNP in 1990. The country's two largest trading partners are the European Union and the United States; Israel has free trade agreements with both. Israel's economic relations with the Union are close. Exports to the Union accounted in 1991 for 36% of total exports, and imports from the Union accounted for 48% of total imports.

The agreement with the Union was signed in 1975, allowing most Israeli manufacturers to sell their products on the Union market without tariff or quota restrictions since the late 1970s. Tariffs on imports from the Union have been eliminated since the beginning of 1990. Nonetheless, the agreement focuses mainly on tariffs and quotas and is only marginally concerned with other types of non-tariff barriers. Although the Free Trade Area Agreement improves Israel's position in the Union *vis-à-vis* other third countries, it does not offer equal terms to the country's companies competing with Union-based firms in their home markets.

The analysis in the preceding sections indicates that, despite the Free Trade Area Agreement between Israel and the Union, Israeli firms competing in Union markets are going to be affected by the pending changes. It would therefore be expected that Israeli firms will increase their use of international strategic alliances in the Union towards 1993.

In order to study the response of Israeli outsider firms to EC92, data were gathered at the firm level regarding the firms' interpretation and response to EC92. Eighty four Israeli manufacturers, exporters to the Union, participated in the study. This sample includes nearly all major Israeli manufacturers operating in the Union market, as well as a random sample of smaller exporters (defined as firms with overall sales reached USD 5 million or less in 1990). Data were gathered during 1991 by means of structured interviews as well as mailed questionnaires. Information was provided either by the CEO or by senior managers.

Table 35. Descriptive statistics of the firms in the sample

	Range	**Median**
Year of establishment	1924 - 1990	1968
No. of employees	3 - 3000	235
Export started	1946 - 1990	1976
Export to EC started	1951 - 1990	1979
Sales total*	1 - 305	26
Exports*	0.6 - 260	13
Sales in EC*	0.1 - 110	7

*In the year 1990, figures in millions of USD.

Firms from nine different manufacturing industries participated, including food and beverages, textiles and clothing, rubber and plastic, chemicals and petroleum, metal and metal products, electrical products and electronics, jewelry, medical and optical equipment. The above constitute Israel's manufacturing export industries.

Descriptive statistics regarding the sample are presented in Table 35.

The 84 firms were divided into two categories: firms that have international strategic alliances in the Union and firms that do not. Firms were categorized as employing international strategic alliances if they reported that they had an alliance in the Union or were in the process of setting up an international strategic alliance that would start operating before the year 1993.

Five types of international strategic alliances were examined.

- *International minority holdings* – alliances set up between two existing firms, where the Israeli firm holds less than 50% of the shares of an Union-based firm.
- *International joint ventures (IJVs)* – separate ventures established and jointly owned by at least two parent firms, one an Israeli and one an Union-based firm.
- *An international cooperation agreement* – an agreement that involves cooperation in a certain functional field, between an Israeli and Union-based firm for an unlimited period. This type of cooperation does not involve investment in shares. Cooperation often involves production or marketing.
- *An international project* – an alliance based on cooperation in

Table 36. International strategic alliances set up by Israeli firms in the European Community.

Types	Before 1987	1987-1990	1990-1993
International joint venture	3	1	19
Minority holding	0	0	6
Cooperative agreement	1	2	17
Project	1	0	13
Know-how exchange	0	1	4
Total*	5	4	59

*Some firms employed different types of international strategic alliancess simultaneously.

one specific project, usually for a limited period. This type of alliance is typical for international strategic alliances in research and development.

• *International know-how exchange* – an alliance with relatively limited involvement over time. The firms exchange know-how in a certain area, after which the relationship may be ended.

Figures presented in Table 36 show a marked increase in the use of international strategic alliances between 1990 and 1993. However, not all types of alliances seem to be considered equally attractive. International joint ventures are the most common type of international strategic alliances sought. When all forms of international strategic alliances are viewed as one type of strategic response, approximately 50% of the firms studied (44 firms) were employing or planning to employ at least one type of international strategic alliance in the Union before 1993.

We will focus on the 44 firms that indicated that they employ international strategic alliances in the Union. It was hypothesized in the previous section that firms will tend to use international strategic alliances more frequently when environmental changes are perceived. Based on the theoretical discussion, it is expected that a positive relationship will be found between perceived environmental change and the use of international strategic alliances by Israeli firms in the Union. It was further argued that interpretation of new opportunities or threats leads firms to use interna-

Table 37. Relationships between the use of international strategies alliances, perceived environmental change, and perceived opportunities and threats.

Source	chi square	df	P<
Perceived overall change	5.59	1	0.02
Change in opportunities/threats	2.22	1	0.14

tional strategic alliances. Thus a positive relationship is expected to be found between the interpreted opportunities and threats and the use of international strategic alliances.

Cross-tabulation shows a positive relationship between the degree of perceived overall environmental change and the use of international strategic alliances as a strategic response. The relationship has a chi-square of 5.59 and is significant at the *P*<.02 level (Table 37). The division of cases within the cells shows that when change in the Union environment is perceived to be high, the majority of firms prefer to use international strategic alliances. When environmental change is perceived to be low, the majority of firms do not employ alliances. In other words, international strategic alliances are perceived as a viable strategy to cope with change in the Union environment.

Cross-tabulation further shows that firms that perceive a change in opportunities and/or threats as a result of the creation of the single market seek international strategic alliances more frequently than firms that do not perceive any changes in opportunities or threats. However, the difference between the two groups is not statistically significant. Table 37 summarizes the results.

What motivates outsider firms to use international strategic alliances rather than other international strategies in response to EC92? The strategic behavior school suggested that firms will prefer to use international strategic alliances when this allows them to exploit additional resources that would be difficult to obtain on their own. EC92 creates a situation in which it is difficult for small firms to compete in the whole market. Israeli firms operating in the Union are small compared with many other international firms. Because of their size, it is relatively difficult for most Israeli firms to internalize all resources needed to compete in the enlarged market. In addition, it is difficult for many of the Israeli firms to acquire a good understanding of the Union market. It is therefore expected that Israeli firms that set up international strategic alliances in the Union do so in order to obtain additional resources related to market information and marketing channels.

In order to study the motives of the Israeli firms using international strategic alliances as a response strategy, they were asked to rate the importance of eight objectives:

1) entrance into additional Union markets through the partner;
2) acquiring additional knowledge about the local Union market through the partner;
3) acquiring local Union status;
4) ability to participate in public procurement tenders in the Union;
5) acquiring R&D knowledge;
6) mobilizing additional capital;
7) Mobilizing additional resources other than marketing and R&D knowledge; and
8) reduction of ownership risk.

Table 38 ranks the above objectives. The data presented show that penetration into additional Union markets is the most important objective attained through the international strategic alliance. Other important objectives are local status attainment and resource mobilization.

In other words, the results support the interpretation suggested by the strategic behavior school: the firms in the sample use international strategic alliances in order to obtain additional resources, such as local status attainment and entrance into additional Union markets, that are difficult to acquire alone. Apparently the firms in the sample view their position as outsiders as a weakness, that can be overcome by seeking an alliance with a local partner. This argument is strengthened by the rankings of the other objectives. Indeed, reduction of ownership risk, acquiring R&D knowledge, and mobilization of capital do not seem to be as important as entrance into additional Union markets through a partner or by attainment of local status.

In the theoretical part of this chapter it was argued that firms in Schumpeter and Heckscher-Ohlin industries will respond differently to the changes in the Union. In order to examine this proposition the firms in the sample were divided into two groups. The division of firms into Schum-

Table 38. Objectives attained by means of ISAs between Israeli-based and European Community based firms.

Objective	Mean	Standard deviation	Median
Entrance into European Community markets	4.7	1.6	5
Local status attainment	3.9	2.0	5
Resource mobilization	3.9	1.6	4
Marketing knowledge	3.7	1.9	4
Mobilization of capital	2.8	2.0	2
R&D knowledge	2.1	1.6	1
Reduction ownership risk	2.1	1.6	1
Public procurement	1.8	1.5	1

peter and Heckscher-Ohlin goods manufacturers was based on data obtained from the Israel Central Bureau of Statistics. The data cover employment costs per industry and the percentage of technical personnel, that is, technicians, engineers and scientists, in the labor force of the different industrial branches. Industries with a ratio of technical to total personnel of under 15% and with monthly employment costs per employee of under USD 1500 were classified as Heckscher-Ohlin goods manufacturers. Industries with higher employment costs and ratios of technical employees were classified as Schumpeter goods manufacturers. Thus, chemicals, electrical and electronic industries were classified as Schumpeter product industries, all other industries were classified as Heckscher-Ohlin product industries. Based on these criteria, 44 firms were classified as Heckscher-Ohlin and 39 as Schumpeter product manufacturers (with one missing case).

As noted above, it is expected that Schumpeter and Heckscher-Ohlin goods manufacturers will use international strategic alliances with different frequencies, similar to patterns found in the use of FDI by the two groups (Almor and Hirsch 1995). It is further expected that Schumpeter goods manufacturers, who are presented with market consolidation, will be motivated more frequently by opportunities in their use of international strategic alliances, than Heckscher-Ohlin goods manufacturers. The latter, who will mainly encounter increased competition from existing as well as new competitors, will tend to be more frequently motivated by threats in their use of international strategic alliances.

Contrary to these expectations, the results indicate that firms marketing Schumpeter products in the Union do not employ international strategic alliances more frequently than firms marketing Heckscher-Ohlin products. Two-by-two cross-tabulation showed that 20 Heckscher-Ohlin firms (45%) and 19 Schumpeter firms (49%) were engaged in international strategic alliances during 1987-1993. The difference between the categories is not significant.

Within the group of firms employing international strategic alliances it was found that differences do exist regarding perception of change in terms of opportunity or threat. Cross-tabulations between the type of industry and perception of change created by EC92, while controlling for the use of international strategic alliances, shows that Schumpeter goods manufacturers employ international strategic alliances in the Union to exploit new opportunities created by EC92. Heckscher-Ohlin goods manufacturers use international strategic alliances more frequently to cope with threats resulting from unification of the Union markets.

IV. Discussion

The assumption that the use of international strategic alliances enables firms to cope with environmental change was tested on a sample of Israeli manufacturers that operate in the Union. The findings show that the incidence of international strategic alliances increased significantly from 1990 to 1993. Different types of international strategic alliances have become quite common and are considered an appropriate strategic response by approximately 50% of the firms studied.

A relationship was expected to exist between perceived environmental change, interpretation of new opportunities and/or threats, and the use of international strategic alliances. Change has been cited by different researchers as the reason for firms to employ international strategic alliances as a strategy; the data presented here support this argument.

The data further show that market penetration is considered the most important objective attained through various international strategic alliances, while local status attainment is the second most important objective, supporting the strategic behavior school. International strategic alliances enable the Israeli firms to enhance their ability to cope with the new opportunities and threats presented by EC92. Interdependence, transaction costs or risk reduction seem to have less explanatory value in this case. It seems that Israeli firms use international strategic alliances in order to reposition themselves quickly in a changing market that offers new opportunities and threats. New opportunities are exploited through international strategic alliances, which enables penetration of new markets. New threats are countered through international strategic alliances, which enable the Israeli firms to achieve insider status.

Figures regarding Schumpeter and Heckscher-Ohlin goods manufacturers show that a clear difference exists between FDI and international strategic alliance strategies. Israeli FDI figures (Hirsch and Almor 1995) show that Schumpeter goods industries employ FDI more frequently in the Union than Heckscher-Ohlin goods industries. Therefore, it was expected that a similar pattern would be found in the use of international strategic alliances. The data do not support this hypothesis. No significant difference exists between the two types of industries regarding the use of international strategic alliances. Within the group of firms that have international strategic alliances in the Union, a difference exists in the perception of the change. Schumpeter goods manufacturers employing international strategic alliances in the Union perceive the unification process most frequently in terms of new opportunities, while Heckscher-Ohlin goods manufacturers view the same process in term of threats.

Lack of distinction between the two types of industries regarding the use of international strategic alliances may be explained as follows: When Schumpeter goods manufacturers seek to service their products in the Union, they prefer to use a wholly owned subsidiary. This way proprietary knowledge does not have to be shared with others while market consolidation in the Union can be exploited. Heckscher-Ohlin manufacturers do not have to protect their proprietary knowledge, as their knowledge is in the public domain, and they thus engage less frequently in FDI (FDI includes wholly owned subsidiaries). International strategic alliances, by definition, result in sharing of proprietary knowledge. Thus they cannot be used for the same purposes as wholly owned subsidiaries by Schumpeter goods manufacturers. Therefore, differences exist in the pattern of use of FDI and the use of international strategic alliances. International strategic alliances seem to be used most of all to gain access to additional markets in the Union, an objective that seems equally important to both types of industries.

In conclusion, the empirical results presented here support the argument that international strategic alliances are used when perceived environmental change is high. They are used in order to extend the ability of outsiders to exploit new opportunities and counter new threats; to penetrate new markets and achieve local status.

References

Aharoni, Y. (1966): *The Foreign Investment Decision Process*. Boston: Harvard University.

Almor, T. and S. Hirsch (1995): Outsiders' Response to Europe 1992: Theoretical considerations and Empirical Evidence. *Journal of International Business Studies 26*: 223-237.

Balakrishnan, S.& M. Koza (1988): Information Asymmetry, Market Failure and Joint Ventures: Theory and Evidence. Working Paper. Los Angeles: UCLA, no. 89/18.

Baldwin, R. (1989): The Growth Effects of 1992. *Economic Policy*, October: 248-281.

Buigues, P. and A. Jacquemin (1989): Strategies of Firms and Structural Environments in the Large Internal Market. *Journal of Common Market Studies 28*: 53-67.

Burgemeier, B. and J. L. Mucchielli (ed.) (1991): *Multinationals and Europe 1992*. London: Routledge.

Cecchini P. (1988): *1992, The European Challenge – The Benefits of a Single Market*. London, Wildwood House.

Contractor, F. J. and P. Lorange (1988): Why Should Firms Cooperate? The Strategy and Economic Basis for Cooperative Ventures. In F.J. Contractor and P. Lorange (ed.) *Cooperative Strategies in International Business*. Lexington, MA: Lexington Books: 3-30.

Daems, H. (1990): The Strategic Implications of Europe 1992. *Long Range Planning 23*: 41-48.

Denis, J. E., and W. Burke (1989): Canadian Multinationals: Their Strategies to Face the European Community of 1992. In R. Luostarinen (ed.) Dynamics of International Business. *Proceedings of the 15th Annual Conference of the European International Business Association*, Helsinki.

Dunning, J. H. (1988): The Eclectic Paradigm of International Production: A Restatement and some Possible Extensions. *Journal of International Business Studies 19*: 1-31.

Dunning, J. H. (1991): European Integration and Transatlantic Foreign Direct Investment: The Record Assessed. *Business and Economic Studies on European Integration* WP 3-91. Institute of International Economics and Management, Copenhagen Business School.

Franko, L. G. (1987): New Forms of investment in Developing Countries by US Companies: A Five Industry Comparison. *Columbia Journal of*

World Business 22: 39-56.

Franko, L.G. (1989): Europe 1992: The Impact on Global Corporate Competition and Multinational Corporate Strategy. *European Business Journal 1*: 23-32.

Ghemawat, P., M. E. Porter and R. A. Rawlinson (1986): Patterns of International Coalition Activity. In M. E. Porter (ed.) *Compassion in Global Industries*. Boston: Harvard Business School: 345-365.

Hamel, G., Y. L. Doz and C. K. Prahalad (1988): Collaborate with Your Competitors – and Win. *Harvard Business Review 67*: 133-139.

Harrigan, K. R. (1988): Strategic Alliances and Partner A symmetries. *Management International Review 28*: 53-72.

Hergert, M. and D. Morris (1988): Trends in International Collaborative Agreements. In F. J. Contractor and P. Lorange (ed.) *Cooperative Strategies in International Business*. Lexington, MA: Lexington Books:. 3-30.

Hirsch, S. (1989): *Nineteen Ninety Two Viewed from the Outside*. Working paper no. 16/89. Tel Aviv: Israel Institute of Business Research, Tel Aviv University.

Jarillo, J. C. (1988): On Strategic Networks. *Strategic Management Journal 9*: 31-41.

Kogut, B. (1988): A Study of the Life Cycle of Joint Ventures. *Management International Review 28*: 39-52.

Mariti, P. and R. H. Smiley (1983): Co-operative Agreements and the Organization of Industry. *Journal of Industrial Economies 31*: 437-451.

Miles, R. E. and C. C. Snow (1978): *Organization Strategy, Structure and Process*. New York: McGraw Hill.

Monthly Newsletter, July (1990): Commission of the European Communities.

Negandi, A. R. and P. A. Donhowe (1989): It's Time to Explore New Global Trade Options. *Journal of Business Strategy 10*: 27-31.

Ohlsson, L. (1989): *EC-EFTA relations: The case of Sweden*. Working paper no. 10/89, Tel Aviv: Israel Institute of Business Research, Tel Aviv University.

Ohmae, K. (1989): The Global Logic of Strategic Alliances. *Harvard Business Review 67*: 143-154

Ozawa, T. (1992): Cross Investment between Japan and the EC: Income Similarity, Product Variation, and Economies of Scope. In J. Cantwell (ed.) *Multinational Investment in Modern Europe: Strategic Interaction in the Integrated Community*. Cheltenham: Edward Elgar Publ.

Pennings, J. M. (1981): Strategically Interdependent Organizations. In P.

C. Nystrom and W. H. Starbuck (ed.) *Handbook of Organizational Design*. Vol. 1. New York: Oxford University Press: 433-455.

Pfeffer, J. and P. Nowak (1976): Joint Ventures and Interorganizational Dependence. *Administrative Science Quarterly 21*: 398-418.

Pfeffer, J. and G. R. Salancik (1978): *The External Control of Organizations*. New York: Harper and Row.

Porter, M. E. (1990): *The Competitive Advantage of Nations*. New York: The Free Press.

Porter, M. E. and M.B. Fuller (1986): Coalitions and Global Strategy. In M. E. Porter (ed.) *Competition in Global Industries*. Boston, MA: Harvard Business School: 315-343.

Powell, W. W. (1987): Hybrid Organizational Arrangements: New Form or Transitional Development? *California Management Review 30*: 67-87.

Pucik, V. (1988): Strategic Alliances, Organizational Learning, and Competitive Advantage: The HRM Agenda. *Human Resource Management 27*: 77-93.

Rugman, A. M. and A. Verbeke (1991): Competitive Strategies for Non-European Firms. In B. Burgenmeier and J. L. Mucchielli (ed.) *Multinationals and Europe 1992*. London: Routledge.

Commission of the European Communities (1988): *Seventeenth Report on Competition Policy*. Luxembourg: Commission of the European Communities.

Thorelli, H. B. (1986): Networks: Between Markets and Hierarchies. *Strategic Management Journal 7*: 37-51.

Williamson, O. E. (1975): *Markets and Hierarchies: Analysis and Antitrust Implications*. New York: Free Press.

Index